IDEAS OF THE GREAT EDUCATORS

the text of this book is printed
on 100% recycled paper

Z/83

ABOUT THE AUTHOR

Samuel Smith received the degrees of A.M. and Ph.D. from New York University. He has held positions as research assistant for the New York State Board of Regents' Inquiry into the Character and Cost of Public Education; supervisor and director of research for government programs of adult education; research director and coauthor of the National Achievement Tests; and editor of the Dryden Press Handbooks of Physics, Psychology, Educational Psychology, and Sociology. He was formerly head of the Editorial Department of Barnes & Noble, Inc.

Dr. Smith is coauthor of *Supervision in the Elementary School* and *Education and Society,* a contributor to *Principles of Sociology* and *Educational Psychology* in Barnes & Noble's Outline Series, coauthor of *Best Methods of Study,* also in the Outline Series, and author of *Read It Right and Remember What You Read* in the Barnes & Noble Everyday Handbook Series. He is the education editor of Twayne Publishers' World Leaders Series.

EVERYDAY HANDBOOKS

IDEAS OF THE GREAT EDUCATORS

SAMUEL SMITH, Ph.D.

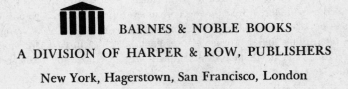 BARNES & NOBLE BOOKS

A DIVISION OF HARPER & ROW, PUBLISHERS

New York, Hagerstown, San Francisco, London

First BARNES & NOBLE BOOKS edition published 1979

LIBRARY OF CONGRESS CATALOG CARD NUMBER: 78-19557

ISBN: 0-06-463480-9

79 80 81 82 83 10 9 8 7 6 5 4 3 2 1

CONTENTS

PREFACE

This summary of the ideas of great educators is designed as a guidebook for teachers, prospective teachers, and other readers interested in helping children to obtain the best possible education. During more than two thousand years in the history of civilization, leading philosophers, pioneering teachers, and social reformers in many lands devoted their lives to the cause of education. Many of their views and recommendations have had permanent value for the improvement of teaching. All of them still deserve serious consideration.

The arrangement of the book is chronological. The discussion traces close connections between the ideas of the great educators and the historical events and social conditions prevailing in their times. Among the most profound and fruitful ideas treated are those contributed by great educators in ancient times, a reminder that history can teach useful lessons to each succeeding generation. It has been said that the only new truths are old ones, and most of our modern ideas on education can indeed be traced back to their roots in ancient civilizations.

Biographical data have been included at some length about those great educators whose personal backgrounds and careers richly illuminate the genesis and implications of their theories. The great educators were prominent in numerous fields of endeavor, including among them famous statesmen, orators, philosophers, reformers, revolutionaries, industrialists, writers, historians, teachers, religious leaders, and scientists. Collectively they represent the wisdom of mankind accumulated through the ages, a source of unending inspiration, faith, and hope.

I am indebted to Nancy Cone, my editor at Barnes & Noble Books, for her encouragement, editorial emendations, and assistance; to Peggy Fagin for her patient evaluations and valuable suggestions; and to the authors of numerous education volumes in the Twayne Publishers' World Leaders Series, the editing of whose manuscripts refreshed my recollection and enabled me to verify the accuracy of historical facts.

S.S.

PART ONE—EDUCATORS IN ANCIENT TIMES

During five millennia of recorded history, education in the home, church, or school has been the principal means of transmitting traditions and practical knowledge to successive generations. Other animals teach habits and skills to their young by imitation and discipline because learning is essential for survival in a hostile environment, but only man has devised educational systems to meet vital needs and attain personal or social goals. The evolution of language enabled adults in even the most primitive societies to supplement imitation and discipline with oral lessons in safety and economic tasks. Rulers motivated by political ambition used educational programs to advance their nationalistic interests. Religious leaders and philosophers dedicated to moral ideals attempted to guide their people toward high standards of life and culture through education.

RELIGIOUS FOUNDATIONS OF EDUCATION

Primitive peoples adhered to animistic religions, which attributed spirits, or souls, to both inanimate and living things as the causes or motivating forces of natural events. The burial customs and cave paintings of the Cro-Magnon hunters and food gatherers in central Europe ten thousand years ago have been interpreted by scholars as indications of a belief in magic and in a future life. However, since writing had not yet been invented, nothing definite is known about the oral, pictorial, imitative, or disciplinary means of educating the peoples of these animistic societies.

Beginning with the development of cuneiform writing by the Sumerians and of hieroglyphic inscriptions by the Egyptians, achievements that occurred during the fourth millennium B.C., historical records made considerable information available concerning the gods, priests, and kings of ancient people in the Near East.

Sumerians and Egyptians.   The priests of Sumer represented the gods and therefore were accepted as leaders in control of governments until in due time hereditary kings, similarly representing the gods, were needed to defend Sumerian cities from invaders. The ancient Egyptians used their abundance of papyrus to create a rich literature, including prayers and hymns to the gods, myths, folk tales, and epics. Their *Book of the Dead* described in detail the steps to be taken to prepare the dead for life after death. Osiris, their highest god, was portrayed as the supreme judge to hear the deceased person's confessions and judge his worthiness for an afterlife in heaven. The creative Egyptians invented mummification and built enormous stone pyramids with burial chambers of polished granite to preserve the bodies of their kings and ensure their eternal happiness in homelike surroundings.

High standards of morality and of social justice were familiar ideals among ancient peoples of the Near East. In Egypt the *Book of the Dead,* with its two hundred selections written on two thousand rolls of papyrus over a period of fourteen hundred years (ca. 4000–2600 B.C.), condemned every variety of sinful conduct, ranging from murder and fraud to lesser offenses such as slander, idleness, and gossip; and *The Proverbs of Ptahhotep* (written by an Egyptian sage and royal vizier ca. 2500 B.C.) counseled readers to follow the paths of truth and uprightness and to live in peace and harmony with others.

Babylonians.   In the Sumerian region of Babylonia *The Gilgamesh Epic* (ca. 4200–2000 B.C.) reminded men that their lives are short, that they should not entertain any vain hope of immortality, and that they should make life as enjoyable as possible for themselves and their loved ones. In Babylonia, too, the *Code of Hammurabi* (ca. 1800 B.C.) listed several hundred laws to ensure impartial justice in the courts, with emphasis on the rights of property owners, businessmen, women, and children.

Persians.   In Persia the Zend-Avesta (the Bible of Zoroastrianism, based on the views of the prophet Zoroaster, 660–583 B.C.) divided the universe into good and evil forces, asserting that justice, truth, and light were being defended by the great sky-god Mazda in a war against injustice, falsehood, and darkness represented by the villainous god Ahriman, prototype of the Hebrew and Christian Satan, or devil.

The Hebrews. In Palestine the Hebrew Old Testament (ca. 1000–150 B.C.) spelled out the moral imperatives of monotheism, brotherhood, truth, and justice—standards of conduct attributed to the supreme deity, Elohim or Jehovah. During the past two thousand years the monotheistic doctrines and significant ethical teachings of the Hebrews, developed by Moses and the prophets Elijah, Amos, Hosea, Isaiah, Micah, Jeremiah, and Ezekiel, have perfused the minds of philosophers and educators, elevating the spirit and inspiring hope for the future of mankind. These great Hebrew prophets, from Elijah in the ninth century B.C. to Ezekiel in the sixth century B.C., taught the monotheistic creed, legends, historical accounts, rituals, and codes of conduct expounded in the Old Testament.

Nebuchadrezzar of Babylonia conquered Judea in 586 B.C. and carried off many of the inhabitants to captivity in Babylon. In 538 B.C., however, the Persian conqueror Cyrus the Great allowed the Hebrew exiles to return to Palestine. Many of them regarded the experience of captivity as punishment for disobedience to the divine law, and their return as an opportunity for redemption requiring unqualified devotion to biblical ideals and strict observance of rituals. Thereafter the lessons of the Bible were taught, memorized, and recited in the open-air meeting places and synagogues of the villages.

Love of children, the brotherhood of man under God, faith in justice, truth, and the potential betterment of society, as well as rewards in heaven—these ideals inspired the Hebrews to depend on education instead of military power (which had eventually failed them) in order to achieve cultural, material, and moral progress, peace, stability, and dignity. Although men enjoyed a superior status in synagogue and society, they cherished and respected women, believing that mothers of high moral character could teach children by precept and example to obey the divine law, set forth in the Pentateuch, or Torah, the first five books of the Old Testament.

Hebrew scholars who devoted their lives to the study of the Bible became leaders and judges in their communities—the rabbis. They taught the laws and codes of the Old Testament in synagogue classes. As early as A.D. 64 the chief rabbi Joshua ben Gamalah ordered the provision of elementary schools for boys in every village as well as special programs of education for girls in the home. In this type of universal education the teachers combined religious instruction with lessons in the three Rs, history, and literature. Following the destruction of Jerusalem by the Roman emperor Titus in A.D. 70, and the consequent need to decentralize religious learning, rapid progress was made in the development of a great body of theological, legal, civic, and cultural information based on the Bible. This work was made available in two sets of volumes: the Palestinian Talmud, completed early in the fifth century A.D., and the Babylonian Talmud, completed about A.D. 500 and comprising about forty volumes. The scholars who wrote these religious and educational works covered an enormous variety of traditions, ideals, customs, and laws, including interpretations, implications, and applications of the Old Testament. Ancient oral teachings, as well as written opinions of authorities and sages, were cited to authenticate the Talmudic information and instructions relating to customs, rituals, and obligations in areas such as agriculture and other occupations, personal habits, holidays, health and medicine, legal decisions, manners and morals, historical observances and studies, folk tales, family relationships—every major or minor aspect of everyday life deemed worthy of attention.

Early Christians. The early Christians accepted the Old Testament and also agreed with many of the rituals, interpretations, and beliefs of Essene, Quamran, and other Jewish groups inhabiting Palestine during the first and second centuries B.C. The Christians, however, believed in the doctrine of original sin and in Jesus as the divine prophet, priest, and Messiah, as God's son, who would not reward only one Chosen People but would prepare all people for eternal life. This view was rejected by the Hebrews except for the tiny minority who followed Saint Paul of

Tarsus and other writers of the New Testament and early church epistles, such as Saint Mark, the Apostle Saint Matthew, the Cyprian Levite convert Barnabas, and the Apostle John the Evangelist. Paul was an extremely effective propagandist and educator, an ideal adherent, partly because of his threefold status as a Jew, a Roman citizen, and a Christian disciple. His remarkable letters and numerous missionary journeys gave the new faith a tremendous impetus. Paul and John expounded and emphasized the unique doctrine of the Trinity, so difficult to convey to skeptical Jewish, Greek, and Roman audiences. The Epistles of Paul, the Gospels of Matthew, Luke, and John, and the other writings of the earliest Christian leaders spread the ideas and ideals of the New Testament. Many common people in the Roman Empire were willing to heed their message at a time when the polytheistic religions, with their confusing and conflicting gods, were on the decline, losing much of their force in the face of increasing doubts and cynicism. This was a time also when the Jews were fearfully attempting to preserve their ancient beliefs and customs despite repeated military defeats by hostile governments, the destruction of their two kingdoms, and the loss of many followers after Titus destroyed the temple in Jerusalem. The Hebrew religion persevered among dedicated adherents, but the Christian faith became the dominant influence on European institutions and culture.

Islam.   In the Near East, Africa, and Asia, however, another religion, indebted for some basic ideas to Judaism, Christianity, and other religions of ancient times, attracted enormous audiences. This new religion of Islam, founded by Mohammed (A.D. 570–632), originating in Arabia, spread rapidly throughout the Near East, Africa, India, Indonesia, the Philippines, and other lands. It recapitulated numerous beliefs and historical accounts expounded in the Old and New Testaments, the Hebrew Talmuds, and the Bible of Zoroastrianism, the Zend-Avesta. In the Koran, the Islamic sacred book, are found the familiar ideas of a supreme, all-powerful, yet compassionate and merciful God (Allah); great prophets, such as Moses, Jesus, and Mohammed (the greatest of them), teaching the nature of God; concepts of good and evil, heaven and hell; high standards of morality, kindness, and charity; and many rituals. Islam, however, added fundamental concepts of its own, especially the beliefs in unavoidable Fate (kismet) as the will of God and in the obligation of faithful adherents to wage a Holy War (jihad) against nonbelievers (excepting Jews and Christians, who were to be permitted their own worship) unless the infidels accepted the Islamic faith. Despite internal dissension and the development of competing sects, the success of Islam is attested to by the vast number of adherents, in our own time reaching a total of nearly 550 million, or about one-fifth of the world's religious population.

The Far East. The principal religions that formed the basis for education and culture in the ancient Far East were Taoism and Confucianism in China; Hinduism and Buddhism in India; and Shintoism and Buddhism in Japan.

TAOISM. Taoism posited a mystical view of the universe as a perfect or ideal system operating in obedience to an impersonal force or deity; its adherents were taught to accept and adjust passively to the laws and workings of nature. The main tenets of Taoism are contained in the brief volume *Tao Te Ching (The Teachings of Tao,* that is, the Way or Ruling Principle of Nature), attributed to the legendary Chinese philosopher Laotzu (sixth century B.C.).

According to Taoism, heaven also has natural laws of its own, but all such laws of man, earth, and heaven are subordinate to the autonomous, self-directive Tao, the supreme law that governs the universe. During the fourth century B.C. another famous Chinese thinker, Chuang-tzu, popularized the teachings of Laotzu through numerous delightful parables and stories. But Taoism as an organized religion deteriorated in modern times and, according to statistics available prior to the Cultural Revolution of the late 1960s in China, attracted only about 54 million adherents.

CONFUCIANISM. Confucius (ca. 551–479 B.C.) was a conservative teacher to whom the ideas of Lao-tzu seemed too mystical and defeatist. Noting the corruption and immorality prevalent in his time, he advocated, instead of a do-nothing passivity, a return to the "good old days" when people were honorable and obedient, charitable and kind, loyal to the family and to the government.

Confucius believed that every human being is essentially good and needs only the right kind of education in order to develop his inner nature and thus become a learned, virtuous person dedicated to ethical ideals, respectful of parents and ancestors (as sources of knowledge and wisdom), moderate in all things, and while not denying a supreme principle or deity in heaven, devoted mainly to harmonious human relationships and practical tasks here on earth.

Confucius was born into the K'ung clan (hence his Chinese name, K'ung Fu-tse, "the philosopher K'ung") in the state of Lu (Shantung in modern times) during a decadent period of the Chou dynasty and was himself descended on his father's side from the royal house of Shang. His father died at the age of seventy-three, when Confucius was only three years old, leaving the family in poverty. In his youth Confucius worked hard as a storekeeper and also as a superintendent of parks, with no desire to accumulate wealth but only to support his family. He was twenty-two years old when he began his teaching career, instructing boys in morality and civics.

He believed in the natural capacity of pupils to learn by reasoning from preliminary information ("a corner of a subject") to more advanced facts and conclusions ("the other three corners of a subject"). People, he said, could learn righteous conduct by imitating their superiors, who would themselves become model rulers if they followed his guidance, which was based on the moral character and examples of virtuous ancestors, the leaders of a golden age in Chinese history. He therefore emphasized the study of historical events and the literature and traditions of the nation. He asserted that if all the people were motivated to learn the lessons of history, studying the consequences of evil or oppressive governments, they would reform their own characters and become "superior" people better able to endure hardships. In human relationships they would follow the golden rule (expressed in negative terms as "Do not do to others what you do not want done to you"), waiting cautiously for bad rulers to mend their ways or for good ones to succeed them.

Confucius served the community for a few years as a magistrate and as a minister in the government. As a social reformer he

condemned government corruption, excessive taxation, and prevailing conditions of war and poverty; his views offended the
aristocrats in his own province, who eventually forced him into
exile. Thus his idealistic reforms failed to transform the regime
in the state of Lu, just as they subsequently failed in other states
during his thirteen years of traveling in a futile search for rulers
who would accept his principles and counsel. Nevertheless, his
teachings endured for nearly 2,500 years. In our own times, prior
to the Cultural Revolution of the late sixties in China, Confucianism enrolled more than 200 million adherents.

HINDUISM. The ancient polytheistic religion of Hinduism
developed over a period of thousands of years during which
numerous gods were objects of worship, but the three main gods
have been Brahma, the everlasting universal creator; Shiva, the
god of destruction and reproduction; and Vishnu, a beneficent
god, known as the preserver, who assumes subhuman as well as
human forms. Hinduism has been the most popular faith in
India, where there are 450 million out of a total of 520 million
communicants worldwide. Ancient religious works of Hinduism,
written in Sanskrit, comprise the following five categories. (1)
The Vedas (four books), perhaps as old as 1500 b.c., include more
than one thousand hymns to the gods, with emphasis on the
worship of Brahma. (2) The Brahamanas contain philosophical
commentaries on the Vedic writings. (3) Upanishad works of
philosophy explain Hinduist ideas about the universe and *turiya*
(comparable to the Buddhist nirvana), the process whereby the
soul, purified by good deeds and faith, is united with the soul of
the entire universe, a state regarded as the ultimate goal of life.
(4) The *Mahabharata* poems, in numerous volumes, include the
Bhagavad-Gita, a long poem addressed to the god Vishnu. (5) The
Ramayana epic relates the career of the good king Rama, incar-
nation of the god Vishnu.

Among the beliefs commonly held by Hinduist cults is the
concept of karma as the means whereby one's behavior in this
life or in a previous life determines one's high or low status in
the present life or the next life. Each individual is believed to
be repeatedly born and reborn in human or animal form (in
reincarnations called samsara) until he becomes perfectly puri-

fied as part of the universal soul. Meanwhile karma fixes his status as a member of a caste. Special attention is devoted to yoga, a method of freeing the soul from bodily control by concentrating one's mind on the self as a being united with the universal soul; pilgrimages to shrines; and adherence to strict rules of diet, marriage, cleanliness, and other aspects of everyday living.

BUDDHISM.   During the sixth century B.C. mounting dissension weakened the prestige of the Hindu religion. An overemphasis on rituals, formalities, superstitions, and myths distorted the traditional beliefs and practices elaborated in the Vedas and the Upanishad literature. One of the critics was the prince Siddharta Gautama (ca. 563–483 B.C.), who was unable to obtain from the Hinduist sages a satisfactory explanation for the persistent evils besetting mankind. After six years of ascetic living and meditation he suddenly discovered answers to his questions, ideas that became the foundations of the new religion of Buddhism, which eventually attracted more than 250 million adherents.

Gautama remained loyal to certain tenets of Hinduism, including the belief in karma and reincarnation. He rejected the extremes of the caste system, which had degenerated to such an extent that only the high Brahmanic priests were respected. To achieve purification of the soul and the perfect state of nirvana, he advocated the Noble Eightfold Path: (1) right view (knowledge of what is evil and how to avoid it); (2) right aspiration (the right motivation to do kind deeds); (3) right speech (avoidance of lies, slander, gossip, and abusive talk); (4) right doing (avoidance of stealing, of drunkenness, of injury to living creatures, and of sexual immorality); (5) right livelihood (avoidance of injurious occupations, of slavery, and of military careers); (6) right effort (attempts to eliminate one's evil emotions and motives, to improve bad habits and substitute good ones for them); (7) right mindfulness (elimination of greed, ambition, and feelings of dejection); and (8) right cogitation (the rapture of contemplation achieved through yoga). This new way of thinking and acting, he said, would eradicate desires and craving for material things and the disappointments, suffering, evils, and ills that result from them.

Even though Buddha lived six centuries before the Christian

era, scholars have noted numerous striking similarities between the traditional stories of his life and the stories about Jesus related in the Gospel; for example, Gautama, like Jesus, was portrayed as having been born of a virgin, his birth attended by miraculous events. Equally striking are the similarities between the precepts of the Noble Eightfold Path and the ethical teachings of the New Testament.

The Mahayana branch of Buddhism, popular in Japan, China, and Korea, deified Guatama, who predicted that a Messiah would come to save mankind five thousand years after he, Gautama, died. The fundamental aims of this branch emphasize the eventual reform of all society as well as individual self-purification. The Hinayana branch of Buddhism, prominent in Ceylon (now Sri Lanka), Thailand, and Burma, has considered Buddha to be a great human prophet and teacher. This branch stresses mainly Buddha's original doctrine of individual self-purification. In Japan, which has numerous Buddhist sects, Zen Buddhism, resembling a mystical Taoism, posits sudden insight or intuition as a means of directing the self toward purification. It urges its communicants not to resist inimical life forces but to yield to them temporarily until such time as intuition enables them to win a final victory over those forces.

Asoka Maurya, ruler of a vast Indian empire in the third century B.C., gave Buddhism great impetus when, after reflecting regretfully upon his bloody conquest of the Kalinga territory, he became a convert from the Hinduist Brahmanic religion. Thereafter he governed the empire in accordance with the high moral principles of Buddhism. Instead of following the contemporary pattern of violence, hatred, and greed as manifestations of imperial ambitions, he implemented the Buddhist standards of morality by teaching and practicing ideals of tolerance, charity, respect for the poorest classes, moderation, humility, peace, and harmony. Although he ruled his subjects with a strict hand, he regarded them all as his children. He urged them to study the Buddhist scriptures—that is, the Pali Canon (Tipitaka) works written after Buddha's death, containing his oral sermons, monastic instructions, and moral guides. Asoka's reign lasted forty years, demonstrating that beneficent government under a competent ruler can achieve considerable success despite burdensome taxation on behalf of the poor, austere living conditions, and close regulation of the entire society. Unfortunately, Asoka's successors were men of lesser caliber, unable to cope with domestic disturbances and ruthless foreign invaders, and the empire disintegrated. The religion of Buddha never regained the prestigious role it enjoyed in India under Asoka, and it has attracted only a small minority of the Indian population in our own time.

SHINTOISM. Buddhism and Shintoism have been the principal religions in Japan. Shintoism was formerly the state religion, but the current constitution decreed a clear separation between church and state; Emperor Hirohito, a Shintoist, gave up the traditional royal claim to divinity. Shinto, which evolved out of an ancient Japanese religion, probably received its name (the term originated in China) during the sixth or fifth century B.C., when the Japanese became familiar with the Chinese language. The religion was closely related to Buddhism, into which it was absorbed during the ninth century of the Christian era. In the nineteenth century it acquired a dominant status as a separate state religion, emphasizing nature worship and ancestor worship. It utilized numerous simple rituals, offerings, rites, and ceremonials in shrines dedicated to gods of the sun, rivers, villages, trees, heroes, and the like in order to obtain from such deities a fruitful harvest, protection from injury or theft, and other favors. The scripture (*Kojiki*) of this religion tells how the gods created the universe, assumes that human beings are immortal, asserts that each person must judge for himself what kind of conduct is virtuous, and prescribes washing with water as a method of ritual purification. Although the creed delineates no specific moral code, many Shintoists are also Buddhists who practice the high ethical principles of Buddhism.

EARLY GREEK PHILOSOPHERS

The ancient religions provided a variety of answers to the persistent questions of mankind concerning the nature and purpose of the universe, the reasons for the innumerable evils and misfortunes afflicting the species, and ethical guides that men could follow in order to achieve goals deemed most desirable or worthy. The founders and prophets of those religions were pioneering great educators among their respective peoples and contributed ethical ideals aimed at the elevation of the human spirit and way of life. Similarly, the Greeks, during and prior to the sixth century B.C., who were taught from childhood to respect, fear, and worship their twelve highest gods, among many other deities, were also taught the ethical commands of the priests in the temple at Delphi: "Know yourself," and "Be moderate in all things."

But the Greeks' appeals to the gods often failed to produce desired results in times of war and turmoil, and contacts with the conflicting ideas of peoples in the Near East weakened the naïve Greek faith in anthropomorphic gods. Influential critics of religion, such as Xenophanes of Colophon, ridiculed the belief in such gods. Some other view was needed to account for the workings of nature and the condition of mankind. To meet this need of the increasingly skeptical, practical-minded people of Greece, a new type of inquiry into the meaning and destiny of the universe—namely, philosophy—began its evolution and influence, which have continued into the modern age.

Turning away from unsatisfactory explanations in polytheistic religions, the earliest Greek philosophers formulated alternative ideas to account for the ever-changing phenomena of nature, ideas based on rational deductions from experience. Even rocks wear away and become transformed, they noted, as do all other objects, living as well as nonliving. What, then, is the real substance of the universe, the fundamental material subjected to constant change? The great philosopher Thales of Miletus (640?–546 B.C.), a pioneer in the development of Greek astronomy and geometry, was the first of the wise men of Greece to propose a comprehensive theory of philosophy to answer questions about the nature of the universe.

Thales concluded that the basic material of the universe is water, which rises and falls in relation to the earth, moves swiftly in lakes, rivers, and the vast sea, seems to pervade everything man sees, absorbs, or touches, and, as a liquid, solid, and gas, continually changes its form and appearance. Water, he said, is the source of power and is actually a living force. His concept that water is the ultimate reality initiated the philosophy of monism, which in various other versions was accepted by many great thinkers throughout the history of philosophy.

Other Greek philosophers had divergent theories about the makeup of the universe. Anaximander of Miletus (611–547 B.C.) posited a kind of universal energy, which he called the "boundless" or "infinite." Anaximenes of Miletus (588–524 B.C.) regarded air as the ultimate reality. Heraclitus of Ephesus (533–475 B.C.) denied that there is only one substance and pointed out that the universe follows a single, inexorable law, the law that everything changes. Another philosopher, Parmenides of Elea, at about the same time argued that only appearances change while the real nature or essence of the universe is permanent and never changes. Empedocles of Agrigentum (ca. 495–435 B.C.) stated that there are four basic substances—namely, water, air, fire, and earth— and that hate and love move them about so that everything in the universe keeps changing. Organisms thereby either evolve into life forms fit for survival or perish. The Thracian philosophers Leucippus and Democritus during the fifth century B.C. formulated an atomic theory stating that all physical things consist of atoms too small to be seen.

All such philosophers represented a new point of view in man's effort to comprehend the universe, each arriving at his own ideas, which often conflicted with those of other great thinkers but were always based upon observations of nature and logical deductions from them. It was therefore only natural for the practical-minded Protagoras of Abdera (481–411 B.C.) to conclude from such wide disagreement that no human being could ever discover an absolute truth about the universe that all other individuals would have to accept, and he asserted that "man is the measure of all things," that each person forms opinions based on his experience, and that those opinions should be accepted only if they work successfully to solve problems but should be rejected if they prove impractical. This view came to be known as the Sophist view, and Protagoras is credited with having been the first of the Sophist philosophers. (Actually, Protagoras was not so radical as to deny all ancient beliefs about the universe, for he himself believed and taught that nous, a mystical or spiritual force, governs all phenomena.) The Sophists denied the possibility of knowing absolute truths and insisted that the proper goal of education is to teach individuals to express their opinions for or against any idea carefully, logically, and convincingly so that others will be persuaded to accept them.

SOCRATES

At this juncture in the history of philosophy appeared one of the greatest minds of antiquity, Socrates (470–399 B.C.), whose philosophical ideas and method of teaching were destined to have a profound, lasting influence upon the theory and practice of education throughout the Western world.

Life of Socrates. Socrates was born in Athens, the son of a sculptor and a midwife about whom little more than their names, Sophroniscus and Phaenarete, is known. In early childhood he was tutored in language, literature, and music. In Athens a trustworthy slave called a *paidagogos* (meaning "leader of boys") serving in the home of each citizen accompanied the boys on daily journeys to a private tuition-paying school. There, beginning at six or seven years of age, they studied the arts, which then included the three Rs and various aspects of language and literature (especially Homer's poetry, to be memorized and recited) as well as music. Discipline was severe; religion, manners, and morals were taught to the youngest boys and girls by parents and pedagogues in the home, later to boys in school; and there was no sparing of the rod. Boys attended a special school or classroom for physical exercises and contests. Many of the teachers owned their schoolhouses, but they received low fees and had a very low social status. With the increasing influence of the Sophists, there was some loosening of discipline, with more dependence on intellectual freedom, discussion, and pleasurable games and activities than there had been during the old period of Greek education, which had emphasized religion, service to the state, and rigid controls over the learning process. Boys who could afford to do so took up advanced study of rhetoric, mathematics, and astronomy.

Socrates taught himself geometry and astronomy. He acquired skill as a stonemason and is credited with having created admirable works of sculpture, but he soon gave up sculpturing in order to become an educator. His student Plato (ca. 427–347 B.C.) attributed that decision to Socrates' belief that he had received a divine command to teach people how to correct their false ideas and incorrect ways of thinking. Socrates had no schoolhouse but simply walked about in the marketplace and other public places of Athens, asking basic questions about human nature and conduct, eliciting and criticizing the answers of anyone who would listen. Since he never charged a fee, he lived in abject poverty, which did not benefit his strained family relationships. His wife Xanthippe is said to have richly earned a reputation as a scold and shrew; and their sons were regarded as rather stupid boys.

In his forties Socrates served courageously several times in the Athenian infantry during the Peloponnesian War, on one occasion saving the life of the noted military leader Alcibiades, who became his lifelong friend. A few years afterward he was a member of the senate and, as its chief magistrate for a time, he condemned laxity in the administration of the government and insisted that the laws of Athens, right or wrong, must be scrupulously obeyed. During the rule of the Thirty Tyrants over Athens, in 404 B.C., he refused to obey their illegal demands, defying their threats to punish him for the ideas he was teaching. Nevertheless, after the Tyrants had been expelled, the democratic party in power indicted him and put him on trial for teaching atheism and corrupting the morals of the young.

The Trial of Socrates. At his famous trial Socrates was charged with giving the constitution of Athens a bad reputation among his students and associates, opposing the established lawful practice of electing representatives by lot; consorting with dangerous enemies of the state, particularly his friends Alcibiades the deserter and Critias and Charmides the Tyrants (Critias was the cousin and Charmides the uncle of Socrates' famous student, Plato); inducing youths to be independent, to think for themselves, and to follow him instead of obeying their parents; and casting aspersions on the gods by quoting mischievous passages from classical literature.

In reality Socrates had been teaching young people not only to think more carefully but also to obey their parents, and he had patriotically recommended obedience to the existing laws of the state while seeking to improve some of its institutions. He had never encouraged the misdeeds of Alcibiades, Critias, and Charmides. Although Socrates opposed the granting of voting rights to people who did not pay for their own military uniforms (to help the state financially), that was a personal opinion, comparable to his opinion that politicians should not be paid for their political duties. As for the charge of teaching atheism, the view of Socrates regarding the gods was far less extreme than that of other philosophers, some of whom had denied the existence of any deity. He himself often referred to the gods and to God without adverse implications of any kind. True, he rejected certain old legends that portrayed some of the Greek gods as evildoers capable of misdeeds like those committed by human criminals, yet he frequently cited more favorable legends and asserted that divine powers had inspired his teachings.

But in Athens it was a time of troubles for old-fashioned beliefs and practices, a time following military disaster, a time of civil dissension and disturbing new ideas that were being promoted by the Sophists and were upsetting old traditions. Moderate intellectuals like Socrates criticized both major political parties as representing, respectively, the extremes of tyranny and unlimited democracy. The democrats, restored to power several years earlier and ruling Athens in 399 B.C., had decided to use Socrates as a scapegoat for the turmoil and thereby frighten off his critical followers. They seized upon every possible objection to his opinions as a pretext for condemnation. After he was convicted and sentenced to death, he was willing to pay a small fine but not to retract his views, defying his judges, and even declaring that they should install him in the prytaneum (the center of government) and maintain him there at public expense to reward him for having served the community so well as an educator. Refusing to avail himself of the opportunity to escape, he was compelled to accept the fatal hemlock.

The Socratic Method. Socrates agreed with Protagoras that man is the measure of all things, but he disagreed with many other Sophists who considered any opinion formed by an individual to be just as good or valid as any other opinion. On the contrary, he said, some beliefs are much better than others, and the only way to teach anyone the better beliefs is to induce him to discover them for himself by careful reasoning. No one, he asserted, should assume a posture of infallibility; everyone should admit his ignorance, then analyze and correct his errors, for whoever knows he does not know can begin to acquire real knowledge. Whoever assumes he already knows the perfect answers to questions can never find better answers. The Sophists, therefore, were mistaken in urging the individual to defend all his opinions, good or bad, and then to try to convince others; instead he should be eager to discover faults in his opinions and change them for the better.

Socrates used an oral questioning procedure and dialectical reasoning as his teaching method. He would ask a question, receive an answer, then ask another question to compel the student to think about defects, limitations, or contradictions in the first answer. When the student proposed a better answer, Socrates countered with another question, exposing shortcomings in the second answer—and so on. Thus an imperfect idea, usually true in some instances but not in others, would be modified until the student found the best answer, the one that appeared to be true or valid in all cases known to him.

For example, Socrates might ask, "Is lying an injustice?" If the answer was "Yes," the next question might be "Is it unjust to lie to an enemy in time of war?" The answer might be "One should lie to an enemy but not to friends," in which case Socrates would ask, "Is it not just to lie to a friend in order, for example, to cure him of an illness?" Such questions and answers would prove Socrates' own belief that lying is sometimes right, at other times wrong, depending on its motives and practical results.

Socratic Principles of Education. This dialectical method used by Socrates became the foundation of educational techniques designed to motivate the learner to think carefully, to test himself, and to improve his knowledge. The student must not depend upon clever argument or convincing rhetoric to defend his initial belief or conclusion, or persuade others to accept it, but instead must find within and for himself a better belief or conclusion. The teacher does not impose his authority or thrust ideas or knowledge upon the student; the latter develops them through his own act of critical thinking—a method of disciplining his intellect and developing mental habits and powers. Eventually the student arrives at the best possible answers to questions—not absolute truths but ideas of universal or nearly universal application that will work better than his initial ideas. This learning procedure never ceases but continues in an endless process of questioning, answering, analyzing, correcting, and reasoning applied to an infinite number of human intellectual and practical problems.

The proper aim of education, said Socrates, is to stimulate careful reasoning and mental self-discipline, which will result in continuous intellectual development and high standards of moral conduct. Using his dialectical method of teaching, Socrates demonstrated that the best answers to moral questions were in his judgment the very same ideals taught by the founders of the major religions, the ideals attributed to divine authority: love of mankind, justice, courage, knowledge of good and evil, respect for truth, moderation, kindness, humility, tolerance, honesty— all the old virtues.

Socrates believed, however, that these virtues must be based on knowledge, not on the commands of deities or priests, that they become part of the individual's character only if he questions what they mean, understands what they involve, and appreciates their practical consequences. What the learner finds out for himself, aided by the teacher's questions, becomes the best kind of knowledge and an unfailing guide to virtuous conduct. Only the person who knows what is good and how to do it can do good deeds; the ignorant person cannot do good deeds because he does not know what is good. "Know thyself" was the motto taken by Socrates from the temple of Apollo at Delphi. Men must know, he said, what they want to accomplish, how to do so, what they can achieve, and what is beyond their power if they wish to obtain the best results for themselves and the community; therefore the unexamined life cannot succeed and is not worth living.

Thus it was Socrates who provided mankind with an effective

alternative to the weakening appeals of religious authority in behalf of moral ideals. His alternative appeal addressed itself to the power of the human mind to discipline, improve, and remake itself. Knowledge, he declared, is virtue; the man who does not merely pay lip service to theoretical ideals but really understands and knows what is right because he has lived through it and has appreciated its consequences will do what is right.

Influence of Socrates. Socrates left no writings, but his career and views were summarized by his younger contemporary, the journalistic historian Xenophon (430–350 B.C.), in the volume *Memorabilia* and by the great philosopher Plato, who studied with Socrates for seven or eight years and was present at his trial. Plato accepted many of the ideas taught by Socrates and elaborated upon these, but he supplemented them with complex ideas of his own in a complete system of philosophy. The Socratic point of view and dialectical method of learning inspired not only Plato but also many other great philosophers and educators throughout the history of philosophy and education. Socrates, unlike Plato, did not build a comprehensive system of philosophy, nor did he delve deeply into the psychology of emotion, motivation, habit, and other aspects of the learning process. But he made a grand beginning in the development of broader, truer, and more effective concepts and methods of education.

ISOCRATES

The views of Socrates had immediate as well as long-term effects upon political and educational events. In the political sphere his trial, conviction, and execution constituted a setback for the conservative group, whose leaders were temporarily silenced or discouraged. In the educational field, some of his basic ideas soon prevailed. The noted educator and polemicist Isocrates (436–338 B.C.) founded in Athens a prestigious school of rhetoric that emphasized Socratic self-criticism and clear thinking about evidence and conclusions to buttress any argument.

Isocrates was a conservative who admired the old Greek traditions and religious beliefs ignored by radical democrats, but he realized the value of effective rhetoric and persuasion as the

means of arousing people in behalf of Greek unity and supremacy. His school served as a model for many other schools of
rhetoric and as a center of intellectual and political influence.
He trained eloquent public speakers, scholars, and politicians,
who spread propaganda in favor of Greek unification, culture,
and power. When the city-states continued their incessant
quarrels, he advocated the intercession of King Philip II of
Macedon (382–336 B.C.). Isocrates believed that Philip could
claim divine sanction for his rule, could unite the Greeks, and
could disseminate ancient Greek traditions and civilization
among Asian peoples whom Isocrates regarded as barbarians.
This idea bore fruit when Philip II, who had been opposed by
a powerful faction led by the renowned Athenian statesman and
orator Demosthenes, defeated the combined forces of Athens and
Thebes in 338 B.C. Philip conquered all of Greece except Sparta,
paving the way for his son, the world conqueror Alexander the
Great (356–323 B.C.).

In his pedagogical work Isocrates insisted that the teacher must
impart high moral and patriotic ideals; question, direct, and
correct the student; and require diligent study of carefully organized step-by-step graded lessons involving logical reasoning
from facts and premises. Along with accuracy and high ethical
standards, which were fundamental, the student had to develop
skill and effective oral and written self-expression. In his own
works Isocrates displayed high standards of well-balanced
sentence structure and logical presentation, which influenced the
writings of great orators, authors, statesmen, and educators—as,
for example, Cicero and Quintilian. But he was criticized severely
by the great philosophers Plato and Aristotle for teaching
students to sacrifice the truth if necessary in order to persuade
others—contrary to the high ethical standards he preached.

PLATO

Plato, the most famous disciple of Socrates, fully absorbed the
teachings of that great educator, then developed his own complete system of philosophy. He founded the Academy, a center for

the study of his ideas, which eventually grew into the world's first university.

Life of Plato. Born into a wealthy aristocratic family (probably in Athens about 427 B.C.), Plato lost his father Ariston in early childhood. Ariston claimed descent from Codrus, who ruled in the eleventh century B.C. as the last king of Athens. Plato's mother, Perictione, was descended from the family of Solon, the noted lawgiver, poet, military leader of the nobility, and founder of Athenian democracy. (Solon was a liberal social reformer but no revolutionary; his division of the population into four classes reserved a high status for wealthy taxpayers.)

In boyhood, Plato enjoyed many advantages, studying language and music with famous teachers; in his youth, he excelled in athletics and became a skilled horseman, later serving in the Athenian cavalry during the same Peloponnesian War in which Socrates served as an infantryman. Plato was about twenty years old when he began philosophical studies under Socrates, at which time he was contemplating a political career. After the execution of Socrates, he gave up that idea and dedicated himself to defending and teaching the views of his great preceptor, whose death he attributed to judicial murder motivated by political and ideological prejudices. During the next twelve years he traveled widely, visiting Egypt, Italy, and Sicily, to discuss philosophy with noted scholars, including the philosopher Euclid of Megara and Philolaus of Tarentum, Italy, from whom he received information concerning Pythagorean doctrines and by whom he was inspired to start an academy for the study of philosophy. (It is said that on his first journey to Sicily he was captured and held hostage as a slave until ransomed.) In 387 B.C., upon his return from Sicily, he established and for forty years thereafter (until his death in 347 B.C.) taught in his famous Academy in Athens, which was attended by advanced students of philosophy and government.

Plato's Principles of Education. Plato's political philosophy, which portrays an ideal society consisting of three classes (the ruling class of guardians, the auxiliary class of warriors, and the working class of craftsmen), undergirds his philosophy of education. He pointed out that people differ in character, interests, and capacities. The aim of education, he said, is to discover the natural abilities of each individual and train him so that he will become a good citizen in a harmonious community, carrying out his duties efficiently as a member of his class. For this purpose girls as well as boys should be encouraged to express themselves freely and thus disclose their true character and talents. Girls should have the same curriculum as boys, with minor modifications. (In actual practice Athenians usually restricted girls to education by parents in the home.) According to Plato, play, games, physical exercises, and stories are suitable for all children up to ten years of age. They should then devote seven years in a rural setting to academic subjects, including grammar, literature, music, art, and mathematics, and to gymnastics. These studies should be voluntary, based on pupils' interests and abilities, inasmuch as only freely acquired knowledge can be permanently retained. For the age group seventeen to twenty years, compulsory military training is necessary. Further study of mathematics, astronomy, and music will be provided for qualified twenty-year-old students willing to devote ten years to these subjects. From their ranks are to be chosen those who will spend an additional five years studying dialectic and philosophy.

The study of literature should emphasize man's good deeds inspired by God, eliminating fiction and mythology and certainly Homer's poems, which, according to Plato, distort history. (The poems were being acted out and events falsified by overdramatized emotions, whereas Plato advocated learning on a higher plane of unemotional, pure intellect.) The study of music, lyrics, and poetry depicting truth enriches the appreciation of harmony, rhythm, and beauty, thereby developing a well-balanced personality and the nobility of character necessary for a just, orderly, and harmonious society. The student who learns to love the beauty in music, art, and poetry will turn away from low or ugly pursuits and will seek to create beauty in his own life. Gymnastics is necessary to maintain physical health but must be accompanied by wholesome mental attitudes; excesses must be avoided; the objective is to establish regularity, moderation, and self-control in diet, exercise, rest, and recreation. Plato asserted that young people who learn from all these studies to value truth, justice, and beauty will become fine citizens, avoiding futile disputes, such as those clogging the courts of Athens with litigation based on deception, injustice, and greed. Individuals qualified to become guardians in the ideal state will be employed as apprentices in government posts during their late thirties and forties, and eventually will govern the state as intellectual leaders and true philosophers.

Like Socrates, Plato disagreed with the majority of Sophists, those who taught students to use clever, false, or ambiguous rhetoric instead of facts and logic as a method of persuasion. He declared that truth, any true idea, is permanent, just as a law of mathematics is permanently valid; as in mathematics, so in other fields of interest, the individual ascertains the true answer to a question by recalling and applying previous ideas—ideas latent in his mind—which enable him to formulate the right answer. All men can discover these permanently valid ideas, and, in fact, they must agree on them in order to communicate with one another. The highest purpose in life is the search for these universal truths. Every student must, on his own initiative, search out the right ideas by recalling his past ideas and applying them logically in his mind to new questions. The aim of education is to develop the mind, not to learn practical skills but to discover truth. Although Plato made a distinction between mind and body, he believed them to be interrelated aspects of the human being as a unified organism. The mind recollects and uses sense impressions as tools in arriving at true ideas.

Influence of Plato's Views. In Plato's philosophy of education are to be found concepts comparable to modern theories about individual differences, the education of women, mental discipline, voluntary activities, well-rounded interests, learning from life experience, learning through generalization, and socialization of the individual. His division of the population into three classes subject to state authority (reflecting his assumption that the majority are not sufficiently gifted to benefit from higher education or to rule others) and his advocacy of communistic control over family life, property, and social institutions (which he applied only to the ruling class of guardians and later abandoned) clash with democratic trends in education. But even these views must be judged in relation to Plato's period of history, when ancient religions were faltering, democratic political and judicial institutions were being corrupted, and the extremely individualistic low appeals of Sophists and Skeptics were becoming dominant in the Athenian social system. Plato was concerned about the effects of political and social chaos in Athens: the breakdown of family life; increases in crime, immorality, and vice; injustice in the courts and government; the prevalence of greed, cynicism, and corruption in every sphere of society. To counteract such conditions he proposed drastic correctives, many of them appropriate and liberal, others authoritarian and of dubious validity.

Plato made many mistakes—for example, in his writings on science, in which, obsessed with the charm of mathematics and abstract ideas, he ignored the values of observation and experimentation and relied excessively on pure theory and logical conclusions from unproved assumptions. (Among the ancient Greek leaders, only Hippocrates, father of medicine, emphasized careful observation and records of disease and human behavior as the bases for scientific hypotheses.) Plato's conception of education as mental discipline was adopted and overemphasized in medieval schools, but his espousal of higher ideals than those of the marketplace and politics made it easier for religious schools to be established to teach spiritual values. Plato's Academy failed in its objective to train intellectual leaders and rulers of mankind, but his philosophical and educational views, set forth in comprehensive written works—especially the *Symposium,* the *Republic,* the *Statesman,* and the *Laws*—had immense influence on his disciple Aristotle, on medieval philosophers and educators, and on modern idealist and realist schools of philosophy. In Europe during the Middle Ages the theologians administering religious education at first evinced respect, sometimes enthusiasm, for Platonic views. But they later condemned some of these as heretical and thereafter bowed to the authority of Plato's brilliant student Aristotle. Some of Plato's proposals for social reform, notably those for the utopia described in the *Republic,* would not be out of place in a list of the controversial issues of the twentieth century—for example, his advocacy of the equalization of wealth and his insistence on equality in educational and vocational opportunities for women and men.

ARISTOTLE

Aristotle was the foremost scholar and intellect of ancient times, perhaps of all times. Mankind is indebted to him for much of its progress in philosophy and the sciences, especially logic, metaphysics, politics, ethics, biology, and psychology.

Life of Aristotle. Aristotle was born in 384 B.C. in Stagira, a small town on the Chalcidice peninsula, which juts into the northwestern Aegean Sea. His father, Nichomachus, who was the physician attending Amyntas II, king of Macedon, saw to it that Aristotle received a well-rounded education in early childhood and may have later instructed him in the observation of disease symptoms and techniques of dissection. Both Aristotle's father and his mother, Phaestis, had distinguished ancestors.

At seventeen years of age Aristotle went to Athens, where for the next twenty years (367–347 B.C.) he studied at Plato's Academy. He was soon assigned to read the great philosopher's writings to other students as an assistant, and eventually began writing his own works, using copious notes on Plato's lectures and criticizing some of them. Shortly after the death of Plato (347 B.C.) Aristotle journeyed to the court of Hermias, a former slave and student at the Academy, who had become the Greek ruler of Artaneus and Assos in Asia Minor, and he married into Hermias' family. (In 341 B.C. Hermias was executed by the Persians for conspiring with Philip II of Macedon.) Aristotle moved to Mitylene and lived there until in 343 B.C. Philip II invited him to the court at Pella to tutor his thirteen-year-old son Alexander, destined to be known in history as Alexander the Great. Philip had destroyed Aristotle's native town of Stagira in 348 B.C. but restored it upon the request of Aristotle, who wrote a new constitution for the town. In 336 B.C. Philip was assassinated, and Alexander succeeded to the throne.

In 334 B.C. Aristotle, then fifty years old, returned to Athens and organized his own school of philosophy in the Lyceum. He lectured, wrote essays, and assembled a large library of philosophical works and manuscripts, which he arranged in a systematic, logical order and from which he read selections to his students. His fame as a philosopher spread rapidly, and students came great distances to attend the school. However, since he was known to be a friend of Alexander the Great and had monarchical leanings, when Alexander died in 323 B.C. Aristotle sensed his own unpopularity in Athens and, learning that he was about to be charged with impiety, retired to the Euboean city of Chalcis, where in 322 B.C. he died of a long-standing stomach ailment. He left a daughter and a son, Nichomachus, for whom his famous work *Nichomachean Ethics* is named. A clause in his will made provision for his slaves and freed some of them.

Aristotle's Views Concerning Plato's Educational Philosophy. Plato was sixty years old when Aristotle came to study with him, and he had already finished writing many of his works. These had great influence upon Aristotle. He agreed with Plato's basic views, but he disagreed with numerous ideas propounded by Plato in lectures. He made his opinions known to Plato, eliciting the complaint that the best student in the Academy (Aristotle) was too critical of him. Aristotle was indeed an ideal person to correct and improve on some of Plato's teachings. For example, Plato was not interested in observations of specific natural phenomena, which he regarded as mere shadows of real things. For Plato the only reality consisted of universal ideas or forms; the impressions received through our senses suggest ideas to us, but only our minds can create the ideas suggested. Aristotle did not reject Plato's belief in ideas or universal principles, but insisted that the ever-changing individual substances and events in nature which combine matter and form in themselves, are the real entities. Ideas, therefore, have no independent existence. Plato's noble vision of a life of pure, perfect ideas could be experienced only in the divine mind, not in the minds of human beings, who can move toward but never attain such a perfect state of fulfillment. Aristotle declared, moreover, that every living creature possesses its own special structure and function or purpose for its existence, compelling or allowing it to act as it does. To acquire knowledge, man, who is superior to other animals by virtue of his power of reasoning, must observe and carefully analyze such structures, functions, and actions of organisms and everything else in nature. The basic principle of education is therefore the collection and scrutiny of facts, an inductive method of learning, an objective search for the truth as the foundation of all sciences.

Careful observation of man and his activities, said Aristotle, shows him to be a political animal, one whose highest natural function is to use his reasoning ability for his own good and the good of his society. Observation of human conduct exposes the imperfection in Plato's (and Socrates') view that it is necessary only to know what is good in order to be or to do good. According to Aristotle, man must not only know but must also practice the right conduct and make it habitual. Thus he arrived at a conclusion concerning human nature and conduct that was greatly admired by the majority of Athenians, who prized and expected results, practical action, from the pursuit of knowledge.

Aristotle recommended the principle of the golden mean, a middle way between extremes, to guide men in their behavior and help them to achieve both knowledge and happiness. Some evils, such as theft and murder, anyone can sense immediately, but in most instances the individual is confronted with alternative courses of action. He should choose a moderate way, rejecting extremes; for example, he should be courageous, neither too fearful nor reckless. At the same time, however, the courageous man will be moderate and brave for a good cause only, for a noble purpose.

Aristotle agreed with Plato that reason should control one's passion and impulses and direct them so that one's conduct will comport with the highest moral ideals, thereby winning happiness for oneself and for others. He disagreed with Plato about the best means to achieve a happy community. Aristotle advocated the private ownership of property (stating that public ownership is inefficient because what is everybody's business in general becomes nobody's business in particular, and therefore is neglected or abused). He argued that the best form of government is the moderate one because it works best—whether it be monarchy (the preferred system if a good, wise king can be found who will at least heed the advice of philosophers); aristocracy (as in Plato's utopia ruled by public-spirited guardians); or a constitutional republic (controlled by a high-minded, properly educated majority of citizens). The state exists to produce good citizens who will live the good life. The most evil governments are tyranny, oligarchy, and democracy because the rulers do not aim at the good life for all good citizens but instead seek their own interests.

Finally, Aristotle reminded his readers that excessive wealth as well as poverty is undesirable and dangerous, that men should cooperate with one another in friendship to attain happiness, a life of contemplation, and noble leisure pursuits. Nevertheless, he assumed that men are born so unequal as to make some of them fit to rule, others fit only to work, still others (foreign-born inferiors) to serve as slaves. Unfortunately, too, in his writings on the sciences, although he made many valuable discoveries—for example, in his observation and classification of animals—he also made innumerable mistakes. Because of Aristotle's immense authority these errors were perpetuated by medieval churchmen and thereby retarded the progress of the sciences, for which his views concerning observation and induction had provided a sound foundation. Like Plato, he defended government control over population, including infanticide in some situations.

The state, said Aristotle, should provide proper education for the children of all citizens. Sparta had a system of compulsory public schools for the sons of all citizens, but it consisted mainly of physical education and military training. Aristotle's proposal for universal public education in arts and sciences was not put into wide practice until two thousand years later when, in the sixteenth and seventeenth centuries, national school systems were gradually established in Germany and other European countries. His proposal, however, was designed not for large nations or empires but for small city-states like Athens, which he regarded as an ideal environment. In his view, universal education should include gymnastics, music, literature, science, and moral training. (Aristotle excluded workers and slaves from this well-rounded program of public education on the ground that they did not need it for their occupations; and he ignored Plato's arguments for the comprehensive education of women.)

In higher education, he apparently agreed with Plato on the values of mathematics, physics, astronomy, and philosophy. The sons of all citizens, he declared, should be taught to the limit of their capacities, which will vary considerably, a view comparable to Plato's doctrine of individual differences. Discipline is essential to teach boys and young men to obey orders and control their impulses. By learning to obey, they will learn how to give justifiable orders and to rule over others. They can be taught to use rhetoric to persuade and arouse people, as well as to inform them, provided that they do so for a good cause.

Both Plato and Aristotle urged that individuals should be trained for tasks assigned to them as citizens and should be rewarded and treated more or less equally as members of their social group but with some consideration for superior ability and performance. Both failed to stress the modern view that an individual might be potentially superior in one type or several types of activity yet be lacking in other aspects of intelligence and skill. For all learners, however, Aristotle prescribed high idealism; diligence; careful observation of nature; and straight thinking. For the development of straight thinking (required for the discovery of truth and the avoidance of illogical, fallacious, or contradictory conclusions from facts or observations) Aristotle founded the science of logic (he called it Analytics), which sets forth the principles of valid reasoning.

Influence of Aristotle. Any well-balanced discussion, however brief, of the life, thought, and work of Aristotle will pay tribute to his extraordinary genius. During the Middle Ages his errors—inevitable at a time when scientific instruments and devices had not even been predicted, let alone invented—were often misused to buttress the theological and political vested interests of society, while many of his noblest goals and constructive guides for human conduct and progress were ignored. Aristotle cannot rightly be blamed for the improper use of his amazing achievements or calculations any more than the first harnessers of fire can be justly blamed for the crime of arson. Today biologists and chemists still search for the meaning and secrets of life, and psychologists test, measure, and scrutinize human behavior for clues to its roots. But all such highly specialized scientists are only building minute additions to the broad, sturdy foundations of the ancient Greeks, especially Aristotle.

GREEK CYNICS, HEDONISTS, AND STOICS

During the lifetimes of the three great Greek educators, Socrates, Plato, and Aristotle, numerous other influential thinkers put forth their own ideas about human nature and conduct. Some of these philosophers organized schools of thought that have ever since profoundly affected Western culture and education.

Antisthenes (444–365 B.C.) taught the ideas of the Cynics: the need for self-discipline and work; the limitation of one's desires to the minimal essentials of living; and the goal of personal freedom to be good and to do good for oneself and the community. Diogenes of Sinope (412–323 B.C.), son of a wealthy banker, exemplified these ideas by living in a tub, begging for bare subsistence, and declaring that the poorest man is equal to the richest, the slave equal to the free man, the ignorant equal to the educated—each unfortunate person being potentially better than the others if he has not surrendered to temptation. Aristippus (ca. 435–356 B.C.) represented a quite different school, the Cyrenaic Hedonists, who believed that immediate pleasures and avoidance of pain are the important purposes of living, irrespective of morals, and that people should be taught the ways to make their lives most enjoyable. Epicurus (342–270 B.C.) agreed but with the reservation that too many immediate pleasures should be avoided lest they bring disaster; he advised people to be prudent, to be willing to endure reverses and disappointments for the sake of future happiness. Zeno of Citium (355–265 B.C.), founder of the Stoic school, advocated the goal of happiness to be achieved through the study of the natural world, control of the emotions, acceptance of whatever happens without complaint, and the practice of justice and brotherhood. The Roman philosopher Epictetus (A.D. 50–120) similarly advised men to learn self-control, limit their desires, reject luxuries, and achieve mental serenity by accepting their divinely ordained fate. A comparable point of view put forward by the Roman philosopher Plotinus (A.D. 205–270) had for some time an influence upon early Christian Church leaders.

All these philosophical schools, the rhetorical schools, and several universities rapidly spread the ideas of Greek thinkers throughout the ancient world. The University of Athens, which combined some of the philosophical schools, was attended by students from many lands; funds supplied by Roman emperors helped make it a great center of learning until the emperor Justinian in A.D. 529 closed it as a menace to Christian theology. The University of Alexandria, with its vast library and museum, built by Ptolemy Soter (ca. 367–283 B.C.), was for centuries a center of research for scholars, such as Euclid (ca. 300 B.C.), Archimedes (ca. 287–212 B.C.), Hipparchus (ca. 130 B.C.), and Philo Judaeus ca. (20 B.C.–A.D. 40), the Jewish philosopher who attempted to reconcile Jewish religion with Greek philosophy.

THE ROMANS

Those who answer in the affirmative the question whether humanity has made substantial ethical, social, and cultural progress over the past two millennia must give credit not only to the highly intellectual and creative Greeks but also to the practical-minded Romans for their unique contributions to Western civilization. The Romans were primarily administrators interested in obtaining concrete results, as in organizing and equipping an army, passing and enforcing workable laws, and building bridges or roads. They tended to value most highly prudence; self-control; courage; obedience to formal rules; simple, straightforward, well-organized opinion and self-expression; and strict discipline in school, home, and public institutions. Using their vigorous practical energy and skill, they conquered the Greeks but were themselves "conquered" by Greek culture and education, learning and teaching the Greek language, literary classics, and works of philosophy—especially Stoic philosophy, which emphasized the qualities of character that they cherished.

During the third century B.C. Homer's *Odyssey* and other Greek classics were translated into Latin and made important parts of the Roman school curriculum, which rapidly became very much like the Greek curriculum for primary and secondary schools. It consisted of the three Rs, grammar, language, literature, history, music, geometry, astronomy, and declamation. Students over fifteen years of age attended the school of the Rhetor to prepare for professional careers as orators serving the public in the law courts and legislative assemblies. During the period of the republic, the Roman system of education was private, voluntary, tuition-paying, formal, limited in scope, and certainly not comparable to the Athenian educational enterprise. The emperor Augustus (63 B.C.–A.D. 14) organized two libraries; further progress was made when the emperor Vespasian established a library and founded the University of Rome during the first century A.D.; and during the next three centuries other emperors occasionally aided and directed schools and teachers. Roman education thereafter declined and was replaced by Christian Church institutions. Nevertheless, under the republic there were educational opportunities for well-to-do citizens to benefit from the study of Greek literature, science, and philosophy.

In view of their practical attitudes and ideals and intense interest in military supremacy and imperial government, it is not surprising that the Romans lagged far behind the Greeks in the fine arts, scientific research, education, and philosophy. Roman leaders were most highly skilled in techniques of war, oratory, and public administration. The simple moral attributes and practical concerns of the people were reflected in the literary works of Roman poets, essayists, historians, and statesmen, such as Plautus (ca. 255–184 B.C.), Cato the Elder (234–149 B.C.), Terence (185–159 B.C.), Cicero (106–43 B.C.), Caesar (102–44 B.C.), Lucretius (ca. 96–55 B.C.), Sallust (86–34 B.C.), Catullus (ca. 84–54 B.C.), Vergil (70–19 B.C.), Horace (65–8 B.C.), Livy (59 B.C.–A.D. 17), Seneca (4 B.C.–A.D. 65), Ovid (43 B.C.–A.D. 17), Pliny the Elder (A.D. 23–79), Quintilian (ca. A.D. 35–95), Martial (ca. A.D. 40–104), Epictetus (A.D. 50–120), Tacitus (A.D. 55–120), Juvenal (ca. A.D. 60–140), Suetonius (ca. A.D. 70–140), Lucian (ca. A.D. 120–190). and the emperor Marcus Aurelius (A.D. 121–180). In this list of eminent Romans. the two foremost intellectuals who contributed most to education and philosophy were Cicero and Quintilian.

CICERO

Cicero achieved fame in an extraordinary variety of fields. He was a great orator, a statesman, a philosopher, a highly skilled lawyer, a preeminent author of Latin literature, a writer of fascinating letters, and an educator. He was respected by scholars of his own and succeeding ages for his versatility and insight into practical and cultural affairs.

Life of Cicero. Cicero's family resided in Arpinum, a town in central Italy about midway between Rome and Naples, and also owned property in Rome. As a boy, Cicero studied both with tutors and in Roman schools. At seventeen years of age he received military training; in 89 B.C. he served creditably in the Roman army (during the Social War between Rome and other Italian cities, which resulted in the unification of Italy). In Rome he pursued advanced studies in rhetoric, literature, philosophy, and law; he also wrote poems and a manual on oratory and translated some Greek classics. During his twenties he practiced law for some time but then, for reasons of health, journeyed to Athens, Rhodes, and Asia Minor, devoting himself for two years to the study of rhetoric and philosophy under the guidance of famous teachers, including the Greek Stoic philosopher Posidonius. He paid tribute to the rhetorician Molon of Rhodes for helping him to tone down his excessively florid style of public speaking. The ideas of Plato, Aristotle, and the Stoic philosophers had a tremendous influence on him, and he wrote extensively to popularize them. He emphasized Stoic self-discipline and obedience to duty, acceptance of traditional religious and moral beliefs, as well as the Socratic virtues expounded by Plato, and the Aristotelian doctrine favoring the use of private wealth for the benefit of the community.

In his public career Cicero became continuously involved in the conspiracies, conflicts, and violence of Roman politics. He held high offices, prosecuted officials (such as Verres, the governor of Sicily) for corrupt practices, aided Pompey in the Civil War against Caesar, later approved of the assassination of Caesar, and attacked Caesar's friend Mark Anthony in fiery orations (entitled *Philippics,* after similar orations of the Greek orator Demosthenes against Philip II, 351–340 B.C.). He made more and more enemies, until in 43 B.C. he was condemned to death. It is said that when his head was exhibited in the Forum of Rome, Fulvia thrust a hairpin through its once eloquent tongue—a tribute to the superb persuasive powers of the slain orator, who had unsuccessfully defended Milo, the murderer of her first husband Clodius, and had made war unsuccessfully against her third husband Mark Anthony.

Work and Influence of Cicero.   Despite the teaching of high ideals inherited from Greek philosophers, Roman society was plagued by problems of crime, disease, slavery, war, greed, moral decay, and civil strife in city and empire. Similar problems on a much larger scale have afflicted modern societies. Fortunately, many of the ideals and teachings of ancient scholars, Greek philosophers, and Roman educators can be found in the works of Cicero available on the shelves of schools and libraries everywhere and need only to be studied and implemented. Among the most influential of Cicero's writings are his treatises on oratory and famous orators, on Greek philosophical ideas, and on old age, friendship, and duty; treatises on government and law; collections of his brilliant public speeches about political issues and corrupt officials; reports of oral arguments for the defense in legal cases; and hundreds of letters to friends, relatives, and political leaders, which provide rich information about the customs, personalities, and events of his lifetime.

In the fourteenth and fifteenth centuries, Cicero's orations were accepted as models for teaching effective language usage and philosophy by scholars throughout Europe, giving tremendous impetus to the study of the Greek and Roman classics— the basic elements of Renaissance culture. The permanent influence of Cicero's writings is shown by wide acceptance of his ethical and political ideas and imitation of his oratorical and literary styles. For example, throughout sixteenth-century Europe his *De Officiis,* a volume discussing the moral character necessary for public officials, was taught to students. His views on the need for integrity were directly contrary to those of Machiavelli's *The Prince* (A.D. 1516), which has ever since taught dictators and tyrants that power, not morality or justice, is the ideal, practical foundation of government. The conflict between these opposing views has persisted into the modern age as dictators such as Napoleon, Hitler, and Stalin adopted Machiavellian principles, whereas liberal statesmen and educators of Western democracies continued to teach the ancient beliefs and virtues espoused by Cicero.

Throughout the ages, famous rulers, historians, statesmen, poets, and educators have admired and received inspiration and guidance from his works: for example, Quintilian (35–95); Pliny the Younger (62–113); Saint Jerome (340–420); Saint Augustine (354–430); Boethius (480–524); John of Salisbury (1110–1180); Dante (1265–1321); Petrarch (1304–1374); Martin Luther (1483–1546); Montaigne (1533–1592); Queen Elizabeth I (1533–1603); Thomas Hobbes (1588–1679); John Milton (1608–1674); John Locke (1632–1704); Voltaire (1694–1778); David Hume (1711–1776); Edmund Burke (1729–1797); Edward Gibbon (1737–1794); Thomas Jefferson (1743–1826); and Cardinal Newman (1801–1890).

Cicero's Views on Education. Cicero was no extremist but rather a conservator of the traditional ideals and values of Greek philosophers, which he popularized in eloquent Latin. Unlike another Roman conservative, the eminent orator, statesman, educator, and agriculturist Cato the Elder (243–149 B.C.), who opposed Greek influence (even though he himself made use of ideas he had learned from Greek literature), Cicero admired the language, philosophy, and achievements of the Greeks. He was pleased to witness and encourage the infusion of Greek ideas into Roman society, education, and culture, grateful that the eloquent use of language had become the foundation of the curriculum.

Skill in public speaking, the principal means of communication, was the primary goal of Roman education. The orator was respected as much as the highest officers of the armed forces. Thorough training in oral rhetoric was considered the means whereby individuals would develop into worthy, competent, and cultured citizens. According to Cicero, to become an effective, convincing public speaker requires mastery of rhetoric, literature, history, government, law, and philosophy. Only a good person, a person of integrity, he said, could become a good public speaker. The orator must understand and practice the Stoic values of honor, duty, patriotism, self-discipline, and public service. Cicero urged teachers of rhetoric and public speaking to discourage excessive emotion, verbosity, artificiality, and exaggeration (admitting that he himself had too often been guilty of these faults) and also to avoid excessively severe, pedestrian, monotonous, unemotional delivery. The speaker or writer should adapt his language to the audience, disclosing the truth to them in lucid, well-balanced, precise, well-organized sentences, paragraphs, and sections. Finally, said Cicero, the orator is a generous, friendly person who respects the opinions, beliefs, and interests of others and defends their right to intellectual freedom and self-expression. Before making up his mind the well-educated person studies divergent views on controversial matters—whether they be religious doctrines or ethical questions affecting private or public affairs.

Cicero contended that the well-educated individual will usually discover some truth in different points of view and will arrive at a reasonable compromise, but never by surrendering basic ideals. Thus, on the question of which form of government is best, he will note that in monarchies the people may often be deprived of many rights unless they are fortunate enough to have a king wise enough to grant them; in oligarchies the rulers may be efficient but may allow the people too little freedom and impose unjust burdens on them; in democracies the better-qualified citizens may be treated no better than others who are inferior to them in wisdom, skill, or character. If a single choice had to be made, Cicero would have preferred monarchy under a wise king who cherishes the welfare of the people (an opinion similar to that of Aristotle). Cicero suggested that, from a practical point of view, the educated citizen should strive to combine the advantages and avoid the disadvantages of all three forms of government.

In discussing law, Cicero's progressive conservatism is similarly evident. Upright, wise rulers should pass laws acceptable to prudent, reasonable people; upright, wise administrators and judges should interpret and apply the laws in a way acceptable to prudent, reasonable people. In this manner the most equitable policies and decisions will result, doing justice to individuals while protecting the community as a whole. No one should abuse his power; no one should be favored or penalized. Here again, one sees the moderate view of Cicero—the golden mean, or the compromise that is most apt to succeed. To become well educated the student must consider all views, understand and respect others, learn principles of moderation, reasonableness, and fairness, and search for the meaning and practical consequences of rules, laws, opinions, and theories.

LUCRETIUS

In his own time Cicero's moderate ideas had a profound effect on Roman history, philosophy, law, literature, education, and culture. A different point of view was expounded by the Roman poet Lucretius (96–55 B.C.), an adherent of Epicureanism, the philosophy of education for pleasure and happiness in the here and now. Lucretius, who rejected the ancient superstitions and traditional religious dogmas of the Romans, wrote the famous, universally admired poetical work *On the Nature of Things,* to teach readers that the entire universe is made up of matter in the form of indestructible atoms (the old doctrine defended by Leucippus and Democritus in the fifth century B.C.). In vivid, dramatic, passionate, concrete, highly persuasive Latin verse, Lucretius propounded elaborate theories about the laws of nature, including surprisingly modern ideas about evolution and the conservation of energy. He concluded that there can be no knowledge except facts derived from sense perceptions, the same conclusion arrived at about eighteen hundred years later by the eminent Scottish philosopher David Hume (1711–1776). Cicero, as an adherent of Stoic philosophy, believed in self-discipline, civic duty, the immortality of the soul, and practical morality under a divine Providence, but he could also appreciate the truths in other philosophies, and he respected Lucretius, calling him a great artist, a genius. In contrast to Cicero, the passionate poet Lucretius had little influence in the Roman world during his own lifetime; however, his basic scientific ideas were highly praised by numerous modern philosophers and scientists, including Thomas Hobbes, Montaigne, Voltaire, Rousseau, Isaac Newton, Lord Kelvin, and Albert Einstein, and his materialistic views were accepted by socialist political philosophers, such as Karl Marx (1818–1883).

QUINTILIAN

During the century following the death of the highly competent dictator Augustus in A.D. 14, many autocratic rulers of the Roman Empire were suspicious of orators and authors and severely restricted freedom of expression. Nevertheless, the teaching of rhetoric remained the core of the educational system, even though in practice the old spirit and ideals of the republic were soon displaced by narrow formality and pedantry far removed from the lives and cultural needs of the people. During this period Quintilian—Roman teacher, scholar, lawyer, literary critic, and foremost educationist of ancient times—wrote his epochal *The Training of an Orator*. In this composite volume of twelve books published nearly nineteen hundred years ago, he set forth the best ideas of the great Greek and Roman philosophers and educators concerning the aims and principles of education; analyzed the learning process; and described and evaluated the objectives, curricula, and methods of teaching in Greek and Roman schools, making numerous valuable recommendations for the improvement of instruction. Some of his analyses and suggestions are quite relevant to educational programs today.

Life and Work of Quintilian. Quintilian was born at Calagurris in northeastern Spain about A.D. 35. His father was a respected teacher of rhetoric in Rome, and Quintilian received an excellent education in that city. He then returned to Spain to teach rhetoric. At that time Galba, governor of Spain, became involved in successful maneuvers to replace Nero as emperor and in A.D. 68 brought Quintilian back to Rome with him. Galba ruled about six months before being murdered. Quintilian re-

mained in Rome, where he served as head of the leading school
of oratory until his retirement about twenty years later.

Quintilian's favorite teacher was a well-known orator and
attorney, the clever, witty, but unscrupulous Domitius Afer of
Nimes in southern France. Afer was appointed consul during the
reign of Caligula (A.D. 37–41). In Rome there had been considerable deterioration from the high standards of rhetoric and education that had prevailed during Cicero's time. Quintilian admired
his teacher's educational methods and oratorical skills and shared
his high opinion of Cicero as the ideal orator to emulate. In his
own book Quintilian quoted Afer and cited two of Afer's textbooks as excellent references. He deplored the time wasted by
students and orators on physical exercise, travel to the country
for recreation, immoral pastimes, drinking too much wine, and
similar pleasures.

Quintilian's career received strong impetus when the emperor
Vespasian (A.D. 69–79) appropriated funds for his work, the first
time this had been done by a Roman emperor for any school of
rhetoric. The school became a popular center attended by future
notables of the Roman courts, army, and government. Quintilian
also continued to practice law, on one occasion defending
Berenice, the Jewish princess, mistress of the emperor Titus, and
was apparently well-to-do. Upon retiring from his school and
law practice (probably about A.D. 88), he began the task of writing
his masterpiece, *The Education of an Orator*. Some time later the
emperor Domitian (A.D. 81–96) employed him to tutor his two
grandnephews. Quintilian was awarded the rank of consul.

Unlike Cicero, whom he taught his students to emulate,
Quintilian avoided the pitfalls of politics. It is not surprising
that the emperor Vespasian approved of Quintilian, who followed Cicero in advocating monarchy under a wise king. But the
policy of moderation changed during the reign of Domitian. The
despotic Domitian (second son of Vespasian) in A.D. 93 crushed
civil liberties and freedom of expression and persecuted dissenters
(Jews and Christians) who refused to worship the emperor and
the Roman gods. In fear of repression or worse, the famous
historian Tacitus ceased writing during the fifteen years of

Domitian's rule. But Quintilian, indebted to Domitian (whom he praised very briefly) and certainly no revolutionary in any case, continued his quiet efforts to teach ideals of tolerance, morality, and culture. His *The Education of an Orator* was published about A.D. 95.

The date of Quintilian's death is unknown. Domitian's grand-nephews, whom he tutored, were not destined to succeed to the throne, for Domitian was murdered in A.D. 96 and a liberal emperor, Nerva, undertook the task of building a more equitable and peaceful society.

Quintilian's Ideas on Education.   Quintilian was a vigorous advocate of public school education. Well-to-do citizens had a choice between employing private tutors in the home or sending their sons to tuition-paying schools. At a time when corruption was widespread among public servants and the professions, parents might prefer to keep their children at home for tutoring instead of risking attendance at school with undesirable companions. Quintilian argued that evil conduct could be learned easily at home, whereas a school could employ the best teacher for a large group of students and in this way prevent or correct bad habits while teaching subject matter more efficiently than tutors in the home. Furthermore, competition among students would challenge them, and they could learn to get along well with other people.

Quintilian opposed corporal punishment, reasoning that an efficient teacher can discipline boys in much better ways. Flogging a boy will only harden him, make him resentful and cruel, and create disrespect instead of respect for the teacher. Boys should be honestly praised for their achievements and criticized for mis-behavior or mistakes. The teacher must display good will and interest in students' problems and progress.

The teacher should regularly question pupils about subject matter, evaluating their ability to grasp information quickly and to retain it. Allowance must be made for individual differences in the ability to learn. Teachers should strive to keep students interested in learning, encouraging them to show what they can do but not allowing them to boast, for modesty and respect for others are essential.

There is no substitute, said Quintilian, for systematic step-by-step mastery of basic subjects, such as spelling, reading, and writing. Repetition and exercise of the memory are necessary. Lessons should begin with simpler elements and go on slowly to more difficult ones; speed will come later, with practice. The world of books provides a rich source of information. Greek and Latin languages and works of literature should be studied thoroughly, for they constitute the foundations of a good education. Teachers should insist on the correct use of language orally and in writing. Music, too, is of great value for its rhythmic qualities and its power to stir the emotions and spirit, also to create an atmosphere of peace and quiet. From mathematics the student will learn how to reason logically from premises to conclusions, how to begin with a known fact and use it to clarify an uncertain conclusion or result.

Quintilian advocated early childhood education in home and school. At first, nurses, tutors, and teachers should provide informal instruction through games and recreation, but if even the youngest child wants to advance more rapidly, he should be permitted to do so. Boys will often surprise parents and teachers by their ability to work hard and well. Above all, said Quintilian, it is not mere acquisition of facts that is important, but the habit of logical reasoning. The educated man is a good human being who thinks clearly and uses good judgment. The student should be given models to emulate, ideal personalities, such as statesmen of fine character and achievement, men who have displayed courage and the ability to control their impulses throughout their careers. For this reason the classics should be studied, eliminating crude or childish reading materials too common in homes and schools. Reading, rereading, listening, analyzing, and evaluating what is being read are the best ways to master the significant elements of great literature; therefore it is a mistake to break up literature into word lists or separate aspects, although students can be encouraged to enlarge their vocabularies through practice in writing.

Influence of Quintilian and Seneca. Quintilian's book was the first comprehensive survey of the principles and problems of education. It won the approval of public officials and leading citizens during his lifetime. But many young people preferred the ideas of the statesman, lawyer, and tragedian Seneca the Younger (4 B.C.–A.D. 65), a Stoic philosopher who preached the brotherhood of man, human equality, and ethical doctrines strikingly like those of the early Christians. During Quintilian's youth Seneca had served as chief master for the emperor Nero (A.D. 37–68). Nero at first accepted his counsel but later earned a reputation as a multiple murderer and evil despot who finally condemned Seneca to death. Seneca had taught students of oratory and law to keep their real motives to themselves and to use clever rhetorical devices, exaggeration, and vivid, dramatic arguments, not the restrained, well-balanced style of Quintilian. The latter blamed Seneca for lowering educational standards and, while praising Seneca's personal ability, warned that he was a bad model to emulate.

Quintilian had a low opinion of the contemporary philosophers, whom he portrayed as superficial thinkers and undesirable citizens. Both Quintilian and Seneca had many disciples. Their influence continued throughout the later Middle Ages, the Renaissance, and subsequent times. Educators favoring a circumspect, gradual, moderate, or conservative approach to problems of education tended to follow Quintilian, whereas those who sought drastic changes and quick results preferred Seneca's point of view. Among Quintilian's admirers were famous intellectual leaders during medieval and modern times, including Petrarch (1304–1374), Guarino da Verona (1370–1460), Vittorino da Feltre (1378–1446), Desiderius Erasmus (1466–1536), Martin Luther (1483–1546), Richard Mulcaster (1530–1611), Ben Jonson (1573–1637), John Milton (1608–1674), Alexander Pope (1688–1744), Thomas Babington Macaulay (1800–1859), Benjamin Disraeli (1804–1881), and John Stuart Mill (1806–1873). On the other hand, Seneca's passionate ethical declarations (for example, "No man is good without God," "All men should be free and equal") and the violent literary style in his tragedies, depicting cruel and bloodthirsty characters, appealed to young people, to the early Christians, and later to Elizabethan educators and writers. Shakespeare, however, was genius enough to tone down in his plays the speech and sentiments of Seneca's heroes.

In the fourteenth century Petrarch, who strove to free the individual student from excessively rigid Church controls, made good use of a fragmentary copy of Quintilian's volume; then his associate in Florence, Poggio Bracciolini, during the Council of Constance found an entire copy of the book in a Swiss monastery. The book was soon printed again. Thereafter many of the school curricula and methods of teaching advocated by Quintilian were adopted widely in Renaissance schools.

EARLY CHRISTIAN EDUCATORS

The decline of the Roman Empire was hastened by the corruption, secret police, assassinations, waste, and extravagance of many emperors, dependence on slave labor, luxurious living of the rich, extreme burdens on the middle and poor classes, heavy taxation, and the use of a tremendous bureaucracy to control the peoples of the empire. Insurrections, invasions, a steady decline in the slave population, class conflicts, hordes of unemployed men supported by the public treasury, and vain attempts to stem the tide of destruction by controlling in detail the labor and lives of workers and farmers multiplied the complex problems of governments and governed alike. Scholars have devoted endless time to analyses of the long-term causes for the decline and fall of the Roman Empire, but among the decisive immediate causes were the tyranny and brutality of the emperors and their agents. Imperial policies antagonized victims and friends of victims while failing to strengthen the confidence and loyalty of subjected peoples.

In the year 330 the empire was divided; in 410 the Gothic conqueror Alaric captured and plundered Rome; finally, in 476 the German military leader Odoacer (then serving as counselor to the West Roman Emperor Romulus Augustulus) seized the throne, ending the empire in the West. (The empire in the East, however, survived for one thousand years under Christian emperors and patriarchs until the capture of Constantinople by the Turks in 1453.) The pessimistic view of Seneca that slavery, inequality, and autocracy would be disastrous to the empire proved to be more valid than the defense of slavery, inequality, and monarchy by Aristotle and other ancient philosophers. In any case, given the structure and character of society in the West Roman Empire, disaster became readily predictable if not inevitable.

Meanwhile, as the power and culture of the empire were deteriorating, the Christian Church (given its greatest impetus when the emperor Constantine converted to Christianity about A.D. 312) was gaining headway, especially among the poor and oppressed masses. A new religious spirit and a new type of education were gradually evolving. During the Patristic period of the Church (A.D. 100–400) a number of influential theologians and educators advocated changes in the aims and design of education. Among the leading reformers were Pantaenus of Alexandria (ca. 180–200), Clement of Alexandria (ca. 150–220), and Origen of Alexandria and Caesarea (ca. 185–254), who attempted to combine the ideas of Greek philosophers and scientists with the main tenets of Christianity as the foundations of education and society.

The Greek theologian Clement, one of the founders of the Christian Church, was an Athenian who converted to Christianity, then served as head of the famous Church school in Alexandria. Clement urged Greek scholars to give up their pagan gods and to worship one God, pointing out that the greatest of Greek thinkers, like the Hebrew prophets, had posited the existence of only one divinity or spiritual principle governing the universe. As an educator thoroughly familiar with Greek philosophy and literature, he appealed to many other students of the classics and convinced them that the Gospels provided a fuller development and explication of the ideas of Greek philosophers, such as Plato. Clement's own teacher had been Plantaenus, the first head of the Alexandria Church school, a converted Stoic philosopher; and Clement's most renowned disciple was Origen, who succeeded Clement as head of the same school. These three educators pioneered in formulating and teaching the theological foundations of Christianity, and their school became a model for numerous catechetical and cathedral schools that were established by bishops to train young people for the priesthood.

Their approach was opposed, however, by other important Christian educators, such as Tertullian of Carthage (ca. 160–230), Saint Jerome of Pannonia (ca. 340–420), and Saint Augustine of Numidia (354–430), all of whom taught that faith, not reason, is the only valid basis for the Christian religion, the only source of real truth. Intellectual studies, they asserted, might reveal some correct information or point to useful facts, but only faith could disclose the truth about God and the universe and guide sinful men toward a life, on earth and in heaven, of goodness, spiritual peace, and obedience to the Creator. This view had a decisive influence on the course of education during the early Middle Ages. Consequently the study of the Greek and Roman classics, philosophy, and science was often subordinated or even discouraged by zealous churchmen until the work of Charlemagne and Alcuin late in the eighth century.

PART TWO—EDUCATORS IN MEDIEVAL TIMES

The political institutions of the Roman Empire in the West crumbled during the fourth century of the Christian era. Late in that century the warlike Mongolian tribes, the Huns, in search of attractive lands, climate, and plunder, began to sweep down on eastern Europe. Germanic tribes in their path retreated to the north, central, and western regions of the empire, invading Italy, Spain, France, Britain, and Ireland. The Huns, under their king Attila, the "Scourge of God," continued into central France but were stopped by the Romans at the Battle of the Catalaunian Fields near Chalons in 451. The following year the Huns resumed their attacks, this time in Italy, but Pope Leo I (390–461) bought them off when they reached the Holy City. The various regimes set up by the Germanic tribes that had migrated under pressure from the Huns were short-lived, excepting the permanent regime of the Franks under the convert to Christianity King Clovis (ca. 446–511), in France.

ACHIEVEMENTS OF JUSTINIAN

Meanwhile the peoples of Europe began to develop new institutions and loyalties to replace the old. The Christian Church was gradually becoming a unifying spiritual authority, but in the Eastern, or Byzantine, Empire the patriarch often was subordinated to the emperor, as in the time of the emperor Justinian (483–565). In contrast to the West Roman Empire, the Eastern Empire remained militarily powerful, politically efficient, and socially stable. Justinian's armies defeated the Ostrogoths in Italy and moved into Spain. Although he was constrained to pay tribute to some of the aggressors, he succeeded in protecting his frontiers both in the north along the Danube against the Vandals, Ostrogoths, and Visigoths, and in the south against the Persians. (Justinian's successors, despite periodic reversals, eventually stopped the advances of the Persians in the seventh century and blocked the Muslims early in the eighth century.)

Justinian was a well-educated, highly enterprising emperor, a great builder of roads, public utilities, harbors, fortifications, orphanages, and churches. His most significant achievement, however, was the abridgment and consolidation of thousands of Roman laws into a consistent collection based upon centuries of legislation, judicial decisions, and interpretations by legal scholars and jurists. Roman laws were in a chaotic condition, many of them inconsistent, obsolescent, or redundant. Justinian eliminated some laws and streamlined or clarified others. The results were his famous *Code* and *Digest,* supplemented by new ordinances called *New Constitutions.* This task was completed under the direction of the noted jurist Trebonian within five or six years of Justinian's accession (528). The numerous volumes produced (collectively known as the Corpus Juris Civilis) made it possible for medieval governments to preserve order and maintain the status quo in society at a time of violence and impending anarchy. Justinian's comprehensive guides replaced thousands of confusing sources and clarified Roman laws governing everyday affairs, trade and commerce, family rights, political and judicial prerogatives, and even some aspects of international relations. His *Institutes* became invaluable textbooks for students of law and jurisprudence. Thus the Roman contribution to Western civilization in the field of law continued to preserve civil authority, long-established customs, and respect for human rights and justice.

EDUCATION IN WESTERN LANDS

Theodoric, king of the Ostrogoths, who invaded Italy in 489, was tolerant of the Christian Church. He, too, attempted to preserve Roman laws and institutions. During his regime Germans and Romans lived together in harmony, facilitating the work of leading scholars, churchmen, and educators, such as Cassiodorus, Boethius, and Isidore of Seville. The Roman statesman Cassiodorus (490–585) employed monks to make copies of Greek and Roman literary and philosophical works. Cassiodorus agitated for the establishment of schools and the study of classical writings in the monasteries. He wrote a digest of the Seven Liberal Arts (grammar, rhetoric, dialectic, arithmetic, geometry, music, and astronomy) as the subject matter constituting the curriculum for the monastic schools. (The most widely used textbook in the curriculum, written by Martianus Capella early in the fifth century, was *The Marriage of Mercury and Philology,* a composite of two allegorical and seven expository books that summarized knowledge in the Seven Liberal Arts.)

The Roman philosopher Boethius (ca. 480–524) wrote textbooks on mathematics, music, and philosophy, including commentaries on the writings of Plato and Aristotle. The work of Boethius made invaluable sources of ancient knowledge and ideas available to students in later medieval times. His *Consolation of Philosophy,* in five volumes, was written in prison after he had aroused Theodoric's enmity. It discusses the values and problems of philosophy and pleads for faith in an all-powerful, all-knowing God as the highest good, or true happiness. The work, reminiscent of Plato's doctrines, had a great influence on medieval students.

In Spain, Saint Isidore of Seville wrote an encyclopedia of contemporary knowledge based on classical Greek and Roman literature—although as a zealous churchman, he prohibited the use of the originals in the monasteries.

The political situation in Theodoric's domains changed completely, however, after his death, for dissension weakened the Ostrogothic kingdom, and in 533 it was destroyed by Justinian.

Considerable progress was made in Ireland and Britain. Pope Celestine I in the fifth century sent Saint Patrick on a highly successful mission to convert the pagan tribal kings and clan chiefs of Ireland. Subsequently Irish missionaries gained converts in the western part of Britain. When Gregory the Great, who had been prefect of Rome before resigning to become a monk, became pope (590), he was eager to spread the faith and authority of the Church among the Germanic settlers in Britain—the Saxons and Angles whose forebears had done away with Roman culture and Christian religion in the eastern and central parts of that country. Gregory wished also to win the allegiance of the converts and Christian refugees in the north. He therefore sent Saint Augustine of Canterbury on a fruitful mission (597) to convert the Germans. The Irish Church, which was dominant in the northern region, at first rejected but eventually accepted union with the Roman Church. All these events were related in Latin in the fascinating *Ecclesiastical History of the English People* (five volumes) by the Venerable Bede (673–735). Bede's volumes had a tremendous unifying influence in England over the centuries. They were translated into Old English during the reign of Alfred the Great in the ninth century. The missionaries and churchmen stimulated education and the study of Latin and English religious literature throughout England; the monasteries brought Greek and Roman ideas and writings to students, scholars, and clerics. Pope Gregory was himself a gifted writer, author of eloquent essays on morality, a definitive book on the duties of the clergy, and revisions of Church music, including liturgical chant (Gregorian chant).

Despite the educational contributions of leading scholars during the regimes of a few able emperors, such as Justinian and Theodoric, the level of knowledge and education in early medieval times remained extremely low. Most churchmen were interested in teaching only what they deemed necessary for religious indoctrination. On the other hand, Ireland and Britain were bright spots in the educational picture. Also the expansion of Islam in Egypt, Africa, Persia, Syria, Palestine, and central Asia during the seventh century established significant cultural contacts between East and West, uniting the Greek learning of Christian thinkers with the mathematical and scientific advances of Muslim scholars. In Persia and Syria descendants of Nestorian Christians, who favored a Hellenic theological view of Christianity and were driven out of Constantinople by the Eastern Church in the fifth century, maintained fruitful contacts with the West. (Arab zealots destroyed such contacts in the eleventh century, but many liberal Christian, Muslim, and Jewish scholars fled to Spain, which became a world intellectual center.)

ALCUIN AND CHARLEMAGNE

In Western countries new developments contributed to the preservation of the classical Greek and Roman heritage and the advancement of learning. The main influence in this direction came with the establishment of Charlemagne's empire in western Europe. Charlemagne's liberal policies and the work of his famous educational adviser Alcuin reversed the decline of education and raised the level of Western culture, which was then in a deplorable condition.

Life of Alcuin.   Alcuin was born at York, England, in 735 and received his education at the cathedral school of York, where he became a favorite student of the head of the school. In 766 the latter was appointed archbishop of York, and Alcuin succeeded him as head of the school.

During a religious mission to Italy in 781, Alcuin met Charlemagne, king of the Franks, who invited him to join the royal court at Aachen in western Germany. He served as Charlemagne's chief educational counselor, concentrating on the education of the nobility, an assignment he performed admirably for nearly a decade beginning in 782, when he reorganized the palace school for children and adults. This school was attended by the king and queen, their relatives (including Charlemagne's son, Pepin), and their retinues. Alcuin's curriculum at the school emphasized reading, arithmetic, poetry, Latin writings of the Church fathers, and Catholic theology. The king himself learned to read Latin and mastered enough astronomy to calculate the date of Easter.

Charlemagne's Accomplishments.   Charlemagne rapidly extended his regime throughout western Europe, so that at his death in 814 the Carolingian Empire encompassed the area corresponding to modern France, Belgium, Holland, Switzerland, much of western Germany, and portions of Italy and Spain.

For two centuries prior to the rule of Charlemagne, during the steady decline of learning and culture in Europe, the monasteries had been corrupted or stultified, most of the cathedral schools had been closed, and even the copying of books had been largely abandoned. The emperor was determined to reverse this trend and to reeducate the nobility by means of formal education combining the Latin language and literature, religious and moral teachings of the Church, and intellectual, artistic, and practical training in schools. In educational proclamations (called capitularies because they were divided into chapters) that Alcuin prepared for distribution to monasteries and abbeys, Charlemagne commanded the clergy to master literature, rhetoric, and other subjects and to establish schools in which the sons of the nobility would be taught reading, writing, music, arithmetic, grammar, and religious doctrines, particularly the Creed and the Lord's Prayer. Thus for the upper classes he set high standards of morality, education, and culture, with the realization that such policies would help to stabilize the political institutions of his empire. Within the Church hierarchy, Charlemagne introduced a merit system that promoted better-educated clergymen to higher ranks as abbots or as bishops, and he established definite lines of authority extending from the abbots through higher officials to the king himself as the supreme power in ecclesiastical as well as civil affairs.

Educational Contributions of Alcuin.   Although limited in its immediate results by the apathy, illiteracy, and ignorance prevalent among nobles and clergymen, the pioneering educational work of Alcuin marked a turning point in the steady decline of culture, setting in motion patterns of education that were to persist for five centuries of medieval history. Within a few years of Alcuin's arrival at Charlemagne's court, the Greek and Roman classics were being revived; libraries were being organized in Germany, Italy, and France; painting, architecture, and handicrafts were becoming interests of the nobility; and numerous schools were being established in archbishoprics, monasteries, and royal palaces in order to teach Latin language and literature, school subjects, and Christian Church doctrines. Very few children in the lower classes received even an elementary education, and so the masses in each state remained in their primitive condition of poverty, ignorance, and superstition, but many noblemen and clergymen took advantage of the new educational opportunities. They revived the ancient Greek and Roman learning and passed it on to succeeding generations in western Europe. Classical and religious writings were soon being speedily copied in cursive small letters (the Carolingian minuscule), usually in Latin, although Charlemagne himself had a sympathetic interest in Germanic traditions and permitted translations of the Bible into German. The classics and Roman Catholic religious teachings became the foundations of medieval education until the end of the thirteenth century.

Charlemagne had a number of able assistants: for example, Alcuin's friend Saint Angilbert (740–814), who was a gifted poet; Einhard (770–840), the king's secretary and architect; and Theodulf (d. 821), the poet and bishop of Orléans. As Charlemagne's chief educational adviser and administrator, however, it was Alcuin who played a decisive part in checking the decline of learning among the nobility and clergy, in substituting merit for favoritism in appointments, and in building the intellectual and cultural foundations of the empire. In 794 he defended orthodox Catholic doctrines against heresies at the Council of Frankfort. In the same year he went back to England but left shortly, declaring he would never return because of the political turmoil in his native land; Offa II, king of the Mercians (757–796), was rapidly gaining dominance over the entire region of southern England.

Fortunately, Charlemagne had appointed Alcuin as abbot of Saint Martin's abbey at Tours, and it was at Tours that Alcuin devoted his last years (796–804) to educational and religious work, poetry, and theological treatises. Now he placed less emphasis upon the classics and concentrated on religious teachings and the copying of religious manuscripts. Tours became the great center of Catholic education and theology; through its extensive library of sacred literature and its intensive program of training numerous enthusiastic young disciples, Alcuin exerted a tremendous influence on the subject matter, means, and methods of education during the Middle Ages.

Works and Disciples of Alcuin. Alcuin's important works were as follows: (1) writings on religion, including volumes of moralistic sermons sent to monks everywhere, a discourse on the belief in the Holy Trinity, commentaries on the Book of Genesis, a revision of the Vulgate version of the Bible, and numerous orthodox theological treatises; (2) writings on education, particularly the capitularies (beginning with Charlemagne's first proclamation in 787, demanding general education), textbooks in dialogue form on grammar and rhetoric, and question-and-answer lessons on school subjects, such as arithmetic and geometry; (3) verse and prose writings, including, for example, a long poem recapitulating the history of the Church in York; and (4) several hundred letters, which are extant and provide much information about education, literature, and society in the Carolingian age. His pedagogical methods featured the use of Latin conversation and readings; catechetical, repetitive rote learning of school subjects; an emphasis on the alphabet in reading instruction; and moral preaching based on sacred literature. These formal, verbalistic methods were utilized widely during the Middle Ages, and some of them have persisted into modern times. Their persistence is attributable largely to the work of Alcuin's disciples— for example, Rabanus Maurus (776?–856), the noted scholar and abbot of Fulda, who wrote the most important textbooks used in medieval schools.

The renowned Neoplatonist Realist philosopher and heretical theologian Johannes Scotus Erigena (ca. 815–877), or John the Scot, was the most controversial of Alcuin's successors as head of the palace school. He pointed out that religion and philosophy deal with identical problems, which philosophy should help religion to clarify. He developed a monistic doctrine to reconcile Christian faith with a view of nature based on logic and reason, advanced the study of the Greek language and classical literature, and encouraged the teaching of the Seven Liberal Arts to laymen in the monasteries. His translations of the mystical writings attributed to Dionysius the Areopagite (who lived in the time of Saint Paul) were popular among scholars but, since they contained pantheistic ideas similar to Plato's views, were condemned by the Church in the thirteenth century. During Erigena's lifetime another pantheistic philosopher at Fulda, named Gottschalk (ca. 808–868), was accused of heresy by Rabanus Maurus, un-

frocked, whipped, and imprisoned. The ideas of these Neopla-
tonists gave rise in the eleventh to thirteenth centuries to
conflicting schools of thought within the Church.

ALFRED THE GREAT

During the ninth century the Danes, who had begun to raid
English settlements in the time of Alcuin, devastated England,
destroying churches, schools, and libraries, until in 878 the
English king Alfred the Great of Wessex (849–899) defeated them
at Edington, temporarily halting the invasion. The peace treaty
of 878 required the Danes to accept Christianity and to withdraw
from Wessex. In 886 Alfred captured London and became the
acknowledged ruler of all England. He organized a palace school,
to which he donated one-eighth of his income. He translated (or
had translated) into Old English important Latin works, such as
Pope Gregory's *Pastoral Care,* Bede's *Ecclesiastical History of the
English People,* Saint Augustine's *Soliloquies,* and Boethius's
Consolation of Philosophy. He obtained the services of scholars
from the Continent and South Wales to teach in his palace school
and to assist him in restoring the cultural and educational
prestige of England. He encouraged the study of English as the
principal language, recommending Latin as a subject for more
advanced students. He believed in universal education for the
sons of freemen in his realm, at least enough instruction to teach
them to read and write English. (The Norman conquerors of
England, led by William of Normandy in the eleventh century,
attempted to reduce papal influence and to discourage the
emphasis on the study of English by making French the official
language; however, this policy was not popular among scholars,
who preferred and continued to write in Latin.)

THE SCHOLASTIC EDUCATORS

Not only in Charlemagne's time but throughout the Middle
Ages the Christian Church, led by Scholastic theologians and
philosophers, was in virtually complete charge of education.
Secular education was restricted chiefly to the training of guild
apprentices for a trade and of pages, squires, and knights for

military service. Eventually universities were organized, many as an outgrowth of the cathedral or monastic schools, in the twelfth to fourteenth centuries. Educational institutions were designed primarily to meet the needs of the Church by teaching religion, elementary subjects, Latin and Greek languages, literature, philosophy, logic, law, secretarial studies, and medicine. In France and Germany, important works of French and German literature were studied in those languages. The arts and music centered in religious structures and themes. There was a steady increase in trade, in the number of towns, and in the population of the middle class, and in the late Middle Ages an upsurge of nationalism. All these factors stimulated new artistic, scientific, and philosophical trends, which in later times threatened to destroy the intellectual monopoly of the Church.

Frequently, theologians (and philosophers) disagreed on vital questions, making it necessary to explain why a particular idea rather than its opposite should be accepted. As fierce controversies ensued, Church scholars sought ways in which to reinforce Christian faith and to convince doubters concerning the preferred answers to controversial questions. They sought to harmonize faith with reason and logic. (In the ninth century Erigena's attempt to do this by means of his Neoplatonic doctrines had aroused wide interest and discussion but had been adjudged heretical.)

A number of prominent educators began to develop new religious, intellectual, and educational trends. Their divergent philosophies have been classified as Realist, Nominalist, and Conceptualist.

Realists. Saint Anselm of Canterbury (1033–1109) developed further the idea of Erigena that men should be taught to depend on their reason as well as their faith to discover truth. He asserted that the human mind, although it can make mistakes about individual things, is capable of knowing about perfect, universally correct concepts concerning God and the universe. William of Champeaux (1070–1121) agreed with Saint Anselm that the Church reveals truth, which should not be questioned but should be only interpreted by reason so that each person will understand it and see how it applies to individual things and events in his life. Anselm, William of Champeaux, and their followers constituted the Realist school of thinkers.

Nominalists. Contrary views were expounded by Roscellinus of Brittany (1050–1121), who held that to find truths one must begin with individual things, the things one sees and feels, and then classify these things in order to understand general truths about them. This concept was very much like Aristotle's doctrine, but the Church condemned it because of its implications against Church authority and faith, especially because it led Roscellinus to deny the orthodox doctrine of the Trinity as one substance. Roscellinus and his followers made up the Nominalist school of thought.

Conceptualists. An intermediate position was taken by the great scholar Peter Abelard (1079–1142), known in romantic literature as the tragic lover of his student Héloïse. He believed in stating both sides (*sic* and *non*) of any question and then using logic and reason to obtain true answers and valid religious beliefs. Thus if a biblical or Church doctrine was subjected to criticism or doubt, logical thinking would disclose whether it was true or false. The individual should not first accept a truth on faith and then notice how it works in particular cases, as claimed by the Realists, nor should he first examine specific events and then arrive at a truth based on them, as claimed by the Nominalists. Truth exists in every object and event, in each action, and it is the function of reason to discover it. Have faith in reason, said Abelard, and reason will lead you to the truths of the Bible and the Church. Faith must be supported by logic. According to Abelard, moreover, how a person thinks and what he intends to do are the decisive factors; even if he errs and commits a misdeed, he should not be blamed or punished if he has the right intention or purpose. Abelard's writings were denounced by the Church, which was not prepared to accord reason or logic so important a role. Abelard and his followers, including especially Peter the Lombard (1100–1160) and John of Salisbury (1115–1180), constituted the Conceptualist school of thinkers.

Peter the Lombard was an Italian-born theologian who studied in Bologna, in Reims, and under Abelard in Paris. He later served as the bishop of Paris. He accepted Abelard's view that correct intellectual inquiry leads to knowledge and truth. He wrote a widely used textbook, *Four Books of Sentences,* containing reasonable—that is, logical—interpretations of the theological opinions of the Church fathers, especially those of Saint Augustine. Despite rejection of some of his propositions in the year 1300 by leading theologians of the Church, the textbook remained popular and highly influential.

John of Salisbury, after studying with Abelard in France, returned to England, where he served as secretary to the archbishop of Canterbury. Later he became the bishop of Chartres. His theological views were similar to those of Abelard and Peter the Lombard. He made substantial contributions to the development of Roman Catholic law. Two other famous contributors in this field were Irnerius (1070–1137) and Gratian (ca. 1140). Irnerius, an Italian jurist working in Bologna, collected all the Roman laws in Justinian's works and rearranged them, introducing the materials into western Europe and making Roman civil law as prestigious and important a branch of education as theological studies. Gratian, also working in Bologna, has been called the father of the science of canon law. He collected all canon laws since the Council of Nicaea (325), as well as the important Church regulations that had been promulgated. His *Decretum,* published in 1142, codified the canon laws; it was updated by Pope Gregory IX in 1234 and again, with revisions and enlargements, by Pope Gregory XIII in 1582. Thereafter canon law was studied as a required subject for law specialists in the same way as civil law and theology.

John of Salisbury wrote *The Statesman's Book,* in which he criticized the common "frivolities" of the time, such as hunting and gambling; argued that the Church and its moral and spiritual teachings are more important than the government; and maintained that the Church is the supreme authority in human affairs. The proper function of the Church, he held, is to serve the purposes and glory of God, who established and instructed the Church, whereas the proper function of the state is to control sinful behavior of individuals so that they will become obedient, virtuous Christians. The ruler of the people must protect them and guide them, just as the head protects and guides the human body, and although the ruler is divinely ordained to represent God on earth, he must do so subject to the teachings and authority of the Church. If the monarch becomes a tyrant, he should be killed. Corrupt priests are even worse than tyrants; a good priest is the soul in control of the body politic, while the good ruler is only its head. Other people in society have their proper functions: the senate is like the human heart, the judges are like the sense organs, the soldiers are like the hands, the financiers are like the stomach, and common people are like the feet. Thus every person, from priest down to peasant, has his definite role and duty to perform.

The ideas of Irnerius, Gratian, and John of Salisbury remained influential throughout the Middle Ages. The ideas of all the Scholastic educators were finally analyzed, amplified, and synthesized by Albertus Magnus (1193–1280) and Saint Thomas Aquinas (1225–1274) into an eclectic system of thought, which has been further elaborated and has endured in the Roman Catholic Church to this day.

ALBERTUS MAGNUS

Albertus Magnus (Albert the Great) was a German Dominican friar, one of the foremost scholars of medieval times, a prolific writer on philosophical, theological, and scientific subjects. His philosophy was largely consistent with the works of Aristotle, but he did not hesitate to differ from Aristotle whenever his own scientific observations in physics, chemistry, or biology indicated errors in Aristotelian writings.

Albertus searched for the laws of nature, for natural causes, to explain why things happen as they do. He paraphrased and wrote commentaries on Aristotle's works, although he knew little Greek and the translations available to him were imperfect. Previously a number of Arab and Jewish scholars had written commentaries based on translations from the Greek. Avicenna of Bokhara (980–1037), a famous Arab physician who wrote scientific textbooks and medical works (notably *The Canon,* an authoritative medical guide for five centuries), summarized and interpreted Aristotle's philosophy. The Jewish philosopher Ibn Gabirol (1021–1070) was an authority on Greek philosophy whose writings were admired by the medieval Schoolmen. The noted Arab scholar Averroës (1126–1198) wrote commentaries on Aristotle's *Logic, Metaphysics,* and *Psychology* in a pattern accepted as a model by Albertus Magnus. The famous Jewish philosopher Maimonides (1135–1204) wrote an influential philosophical treatise in Arabic, *Guide to the Perplexed,* based in part on Arabic translations of Aristotle's writings. It is well known among Western scholars. Albertus Magnus used parts of Maimonides' writings in his own works.

The English Franciscan scholar Alexander of Hales (ca. 1180–1245) wrote *Summa Universae Theologiae* to reconcile the ideas of Saint Augustine and those of Aristotle with the views of Arab philosophers, concluding that God is pure, formless, spiritual activity that gives a soul to the human body and thus enables it to know truths. Albertus Magnus and Aquinas owed much to Alexander's ideas. Another influential contemporary was Alexander's disciple, the gifted scholar Robert Grosseteste (1175–1253), who wrote numerous commentaries on Aristotle, as well as works on science and on Church affairs; he dared to rebuke even Pope Innocent IV, the monks, and the king for their errors and activities.

Albertus Magnus's views, emphasizing the application of Aristotelian logic to the study of nature, helped to make Aristotle the unimpeachable authority on many subjects for the Church. The official views and pronouncements of the Church thereafter reflected mainly the theological ideas of Saint Augustine and the philosophy of Aristotle. With the contributions of Albertus Magnus and his brilliant student Saint Thomas Aquinas, Aristotelian philosophy, which largely replaced Platonic ideas in Scholastic thought, reinforced faith with logic and deductive reasoning in church teachings.

SAINT THOMAS AQUINAS

The work of Saint Thomas Aquinas marked the high point of medieval Scholasticism. Born (1225) into a noble Italian family in Roccasecca, southeast of Rome, he was educated in the Monte

Cassino monastery of the Benedictines and in the University of Naples before joining the Dominicans. He was a student of Albertus Magnus at the Dominican school in Cologne, accompanied him to the University of Paris, and later returned with him to Cologne, where he began a long career as lecturer, writer, and adviser to civil and Church authorities.

Summa Theologiae. Although he wrote scores of comprehensive treatises, Aquinas's masterly two volumes, *Summa Theologiae*, not quite completed before his death in 1274, established his reputation permanently as the greatest of the Scholastics, ranking him with Saint Augustine as one of the two leading spokesmen for the Roman Catholic Church. In 1323 he was canonized by Pope John XXII; in 1879 an encyclical of Pope Leo XIII commanded the clergy to accept the doctrines of Aquinas in preference to those of any divergent theologians.

Views of Aquinas. Aquinas attempted to prove that the Christian faith is fully justified by logical reasoning; he accepted Aristotle as the supreme authority on logical reasoning. All truths, he said, have their origin in God. Truths are revealed in different ways—namely, by faith, which goes beyond the reach of reason, and by reason, which enables men to understand natural laws as well as knowledge revealed by faith. There is thus no contradiction between faith and reason. All truths are divinely originated, even though faith reveals some truths beyond the power of reason to discover by itself. Aquinas interpreted Aristotle's view of God in a theistic manner, as an all-knowing divinity, whereas Aristotle himself, despite some ambiguous or obscure statements, portrayed God as the Unmoved Mover, having no interest in or knowledge about the evils of the world. Aristotle believed that God did not create the world but that both matter and reason exist eternally.

Aquinas attempted to justify ideological inconsistencies between his views and some of Aristotle's conclusions by referring to the Thomistic assumption that faith is superior to and goes beyond reason in matters pertaining to the ultimate nature of God and the universe. A more immediately practical issue arose from the notion that his own reason and faith had found the absolute truth that must be accepted by others. (This point of view eventually aroused the antagonism of the Protestants, who, in turn, became similarly intolerant of dissenters from their own views). Aquinas expressed this authoritarian attitude explicitly in his statement that the execution of disbelievers or heretics would be justifiable, merciful punishment compared with the eternal suffering and damnation that awaited them in hell for their dissenting opinions.

The authoritarianism of medieval Church authorities would have been anathema to Plato—who condemned the theologians and politicians of his time for executing Socrates—and would in fact have been denounced by Aristotle himself, who, as a dissenter accused of impiety, declared that he would not remain in Athens to be mistreated as that city had mistreated Socrates. In medieval times, however, intolerance afflicted religious as well as political leaders.

Twentieth-century critics have accused Aquinas and his followers of applying mainly the deductive logic of Aristotle to intellectual problems while minimizing his scientific, inductive side and thereby retarding the progress of science for hundreds of years. The medieval Church insisted on the universal acceptance of Aristotle as the authority in all fields of logic and knowledge (excepting matters of faith). Consequently, when sixteenth- and seventeenth-century scientists—such as Copernicus, Galileo, Tycho Brahe, Johannes Kepler, and Isaac Newton— arrived at their revolutionary conceptions of the universe, the theologians refused to believe the evidence of their own senses and reason but rushed in vain to find in the works of Aquinas and Aristotle some information or ideas that might explain the contradictions between previous assumptions and scientific evidence.

Early Opponents of Thomism. A moderate form of opposition to Aquinas, and to Aristotle as interpreted by Aquinas, developed in the thirteenth and fourteenth centuries, long before the revolutionary ideas of many scientists were formulated. Among the critics were Scholastic theologians of the Catholic Church, including Roger Bacon (ca. 1214–1294), John Duns Scotus (1270–1308), and William of Ockham (1280–1349). These educators created doubt and dissension within the Scholastic movement and thus helped to prepare the ground for the humanist scholars of the mid-fourteenth to sixteenth centuries (when new liberal and individualistic points of view developed) and the Protestant rebellion initiated by Martin Luther early in the sixteenth century. Education in the Renaissance and in modern times underwent drastic changes and, instead of depending upon the single approach of Scholasticism, reflected three kinds of ideas: (1) ideas of *humanism,* a liberal philosophy of dissenters and individualists; (2) ideas of *theism,* inherited from ancient religions and the medieval Church; and (3) ideas of *naturalism,* the philosophy of inductive science.

ROGER BACON

The English philosopher and scientist Roger Bacon condemned the method of teaching used in medieval universities. It consisted of lectures, discussions, and debates about authoritative works, including some he greatly respected (such as the translated texts of Aristotle concerning natural science, the treatises of Peter Lombard and Thomas Aquinas on theology, the writings of Justinian and Gratian on law, and the translations of manuals by Hippocrates and Galen on medical diagnosis and therapy). Bacon asserted in his treatises and in his lectures at Oxford University that incorrect information was perpetuated by the restriction of education to these traditional sources. He argued that experiments and careful observation of causes and results would correct errors, would reveal facts, and would not destroy but rather would support the basic truths of Christian faith and the Franciscan order to which he belonged. He advocated the study of the Scriptures and philosophical works in Hebrew, Arabic, and Greek to correct the errors of theologians who depended on Latin translations, and he argued for the use of scientific instruments, mathematics, and inductive reasoning in science. But Bonaventura, head of the Franciscans, who was a Scholastic mystic philosopher (later bishop of Albano and appointed cardinal by Pope Gregory X), stopped Bacon's lectures and imprisoned him for a decade as punishment for his dissenting views.

In 1266, however, Pope Clement IV instructed Bacon to write out his ideas despite Franciscan objectors, whereupon Bacon wrote three large volumes, including his chief work, *Opus Maius,* and he was allowed to return in 1268 to Oxford University. Again he attacked the monks and clergy, until in 1278 the head of the Franciscan order, Jerome de Ascoli (later Pope Nicholas IV), sentenced him to prison for insubordination. He remained in prison fourteen years. In 1292, following his release, he wrote a final work on theological studies.

Bacon's ideas, despite many factual errors, were far ahead of his time and therefore had limited immediate influence. In scientific endeavors his approach was amazingly modern. He suggested the feasibility of constructing airplanes, telescopes, eyeglasses, locomotives, and suspension bridges, and his theories about the circumnavigation of the earth are said to have helped induce Columbus two centuries later to embark on the voyages that resulted in the discovery of America.

JOHN DUNS SCOTUS

Duns Scotus, another Franciscan scholar who lectured at Oxford University, agreed with Aquinas that there is no necessary conflict between reason and faith, but he also asserted that contrary to Aquinas's view, Aristotelian logic is not the best means of learning truths about the universe. Deductive logic, he insisted, is a limited, imperfect guide to knowledge. Only faith can give man certainty, absolutely sure truths of any kind. Faith, he said, is not a matter of logical ideas or intellect but an activity of the human will.

Scotus's criticism of the hair-splitting logic applied by the Scholastic theologians and his insistence on pure faith through revelation convinced many other scholars to oppose the dominant Thomistic ideas of the Church. His school of thought, called Scotism, thereby weakened the church's intellectual and educational monopoly and facilitated the work of later critics who demanded other—that is, inductive and experimental—evidence to arrive at truths about man and the universe. According to Scotus, even moral standards are not logical deductions of the human mind or reason (as Socrates and Plato believed) but commandments to be obeyed because they are received from God through revelation and faith.

WILLIAM OF OCKHAM

Scotus's famous disciple, William of Ockham, accepted the Scotist conclusion about revelation and faith and also the extreme Nominalist position that the human mind can know only individual things and events, that general ideas and conclusions about nature are merely manufactured abstractions devoid of reality. Moreover, said Ockham, the mind knows individual things only through intuition, not logic, and no broad principles are needed to help one to understand anything about man and nature. This contention that superfluous universals or general ideas should not be used to support specific facts was widely approved by succeeding generations of scientists, who referred to it as "Ockham's Razor," because it eliminated unnecessary explanations. According to Ockham the simplest adequate solution to a problem is the best. He, like Duns Scotus, was a devout Christian, adhering to revealed truths as divine in origin but contradicting the Scholastic contention that logic could prove theological doctrines. He was therefore in constant difficulty with Pope John XXII, from whom he fled to seek refuge with King Louis IV (the Holy Roman Emperor) of Bavaria. The ideas of Duns Scotus and William of Ockham had a great influence on Renaissance and modern scientists, philosophers, and educators—for example, the great English educators Francis Bacon (1561–1626) and John Locke (1632–1704).

WALDENSES AND ALBIGENSES

Prior to the intellectual revolt of individual scholars, such as Roger Bacon, Duns Scotus, and William of Ockham, against Scholastic logic, the Church had been compelled to face the challenge of two groups of dissenters, the Waldenses and the Albigenses. The Waldenses, led by a wealthy French citizen named Peter Waldo, advocated exclusive reliance on the Bible for personal salvation. They were excommunicated in 1184. The

Albigenses were active during the eleventh century in southern France. They adhered to the dualist heresy that the universe is under the domination of two opposing and ultimate principles, good and evil. They agitated against the corrupt clergy and rejected the authority of the monks. For some time the Albigenses were protected by the nobility and the common people, as well as by some of the local bishops who resented the powers given to the monks by Pope Innocent III. The pope proclaimed a crusade against the Albigenses in 1207, and his forces massacred many of them. This inquisition terrorized southern France until Church authority was fully restored. But the task of forceful repression had been difficult, demonstrating that challenges to Church authority might win considerable influential support.

JOHN WYCLIFFE

Another significant heretical movement began in the fourteenth century, this time in England. Its leader was the English theologian John Wycliffe (1320–1384), who was trained at Oxford University, where he later lectured about the abuse of Church authority and the corrupt practices of the clergy. He demanded that the Church cease attempting to control the political decisions of the national government and the secular affairs of the people. He asserted that the Church hierarchy should be deprived of every vestige of authority if they disobeyed the moral laws of the Christian religion, also that the government should seize the property of every corrupt Church official and should stop paying taxes to the pope. He flatly denied the infallibility of the pope.

In 1377 Pope Gregory XI accused Wycliffe of heresy, but the intervention of John of Gaunt (the Duke of Lancaster) and public clamor prevented a conviction. Eventually, however, after Wycliffe denied the validity of transsubstantiation (change of the eucharistic bread and wine into Christ's body and blood) and demanded repeatedly that the clergy give up their wealth and land and live in poverty, he was forbidden to teach at Oxford. Particularly troublesome to the Church were his assertions that all religious teachings should be based upon the Scriptures, not upon the traditional teachings of the Church, and that each individual has the right to study the Bible for himself and then make up his own mind about theological doctrines.

Wycliffe began, and his assistants finished, a forceful although stilted translation of the entire Bible from Saint Jerome's Latin, the first such translation of the complete Old and New Testaments into English. Among his followers were unofficial preachers, the Lollards, who distributed copies of the texts to the common people. Wycliffe was condemned for his heretical teachings but was permitted to retire. He died of a chronic heart ailment. In 1415, thirty-one years after his death, the Council of Constance condemned his work and ordered his body to be exhumed and burned, apparently to discourage his followers, especially the Lollards, who had continued their campaign against the clergy.

Wycliffe's English Bible together with his sermons and other works in English stimulated popular interest in reading books in English and thus gave impetus to the teaching of English literature in elementary and higher schools. His defiance of the Church contributed both directly and through literature to the cause of intellectual liberty.

JOHN HUSS

John Huss (1369–1415) was the most famous disciple of Wycliffe. Huss was an erudite scholar who served as the rector of the University of Prague, where he lectured in behalf of Wycliffe's ideas, condemning Church abuses and corruption, indulgences, and the pope's assumption of excessive authority. At the University of Prague his lectures offended German faculty members (who resigned and went to Germany, where they founded the University of Leipzig). Huss was excommunicated because of his constant attacks on the clergy. In 1415 he appeared at the Council of Constance in response to an invitation and armed with a safe conduct signed by Sigismund, king of Hungary and Holy Roman Emperor. Sigismund had induced Pope John XXIII* to call the council; nevertheless Huss was arrested, convicted of heresy, and shortly thereafter burned at the stake. But his followers continued

---

* Later deposed by the council as an antipope.

their agitation and engaged in a long civil war against the Germans, until in 1436 relations with the Church were adjusted without achieving the social reforms or nationalistic ambitions of the martyr.

The persecution of the Waldenses, Albigenses, Wycliffites, and Hussites undoubtedly played a part in the decline of the medieval Church at a time of schisms in the Church hierarchy and organization (there were three competing popes in the Western church during the Council of Constance which condemned Huss, while the division between the Western and Eastern churches persisted). It was also a time of spreading nationalism (the English people during a century of wars against France resented the pro-French popes) and a time of corruption among the clergy and continuous conflict between secular rulers and the popes for political supremacy. All these factors diminished the power of the Church, which had become the superstate of Europe, and facilitated the Protestant revolt against Scholasticism under the leadership of scholars such as Erasmus and Luther a century after the execution of John Huss.

Nevertheless, the Scholastic philosophers, despite their inexorable opposition to critics of Church authority and to novel scientific methods of investigation, actually facilitated intellectual and cultural changes by proclaiming that the events of nature have definite causes; that the universe is an orderly creation governed by fixed natural laws established by divine Providence; and that logic and human reason if trained in logical thinking can clarify and explain the laws of that universe. Modern scientists opposed to the Church made good use of these ideas. But the tide in favor of new ideas, freedom of conscience, individualism, and science did not begin until the time of the humanists in the fourteenth century.

PETRARCH

In the early Renaissance the foremost exponent of humanism—based (in its ideological aspects) upon individual liberty of conscience and dissension from Scholastic authority—was the renowned Italian poet and scholar Petrarch (Francesco Petrarca, 1304–1374). He was born in Arezzo, near Florence, studied law at the universities of Montpellier, France, and Bologna, Italy, then gave up law for literature, to which he contributed numerous influential masterpieces of poetry, orations, letters, and essays, both in Latin and in Italian. Although he never mastered Greek, he admired Greek culture as reflected in the works of Cicero, Seneca, and other Roman authors whom he studied and whose liberal spirit he emulated in his own writings, which included love sonnets, ballads, and lyrics expressing his love of nature and beauty.

Petrarch despised Scholastic works and refused to bow to Aristotle as the supreme authority in philosophy and science, but he respected Saint Augustine's teachings and adhered to orthodox Catholicism. He defended the individual's right to freedom of conscience and learning, but held that the Latin classics would not harm but rather reinforce the Christian religion. Searching in European monasteries for classical manuscripts, he was overjoyed to find previously undiscovered writings of Cicero, including a speech (*pro Archia*) and many of Cicero's letters to the Roman patron of literature Atticus (109–32 B.C.).

Petrarch was offered high papal appointments, which he repeatedly declined. Kings, tyrants, aristocrats, and revolutionaries alike respected him and catered to him as the leading literary master of his age, and his attachments to popes, monarchs, and the nobility were often contradictory to the libertarian spirit of his writings and his belief in a republican form of government. But he devoted himself to the cause of liberal education and advocated universal self-culture as the noblest aim of mankind, far more important than political or social reforms. Everyone, he urged, should be encouraged in the individual pursuit of ancient learning and culture. He gave expression to a new confidence in individualism in religion, education, literature, the arts, and contemporary society. His eloquent, passionate style of writing, his wit and subtlety, stimulated popular interest in the everyday world of common people.

BOCCACCIO

Boccaccio (1313–1375) was the illegitimate son of a wealthy merchant and a Frenchwoman. He received an elementary education in Florence from a well-known scholar and teacher, Giovanni de Strada. In early boyhood he worked as an apprentice to a prosperous merchant in Naples, then studied canon law for a few years before giving it up to concentrate on writing. In 1350 he met Petrarch, with whom he formed a lasting friendship. Like his father, who lost a fortune and was reduced to poverty, Boccaccio was constantly troubled by financial difficulties, especially since his interest in collecting and copying ancient manuscripts was a costly one. In 1373, when he was attempting to recover from a serious illness, he finally received an appointment at the University of Florence to lecture on Dante's *Divine Comedy*, a work he intensely admired .

Boccaccio wrote numerous Italian and Latin works of poetry and prose. His masterpiece, the widely read *Decameron* (published in final form in 1353), was a collection of one hundred romantic, vigorous, and lusty stories in Italian about all sorts of people—kings and nobles, priests, artists, lovers, artisans, merchants, peasants, fools, and hypocrites. It was a storehouse of familiar characters and adventures that were eagerly devoured by the common people of Boccaccio's time. Many of Boccaccio's themes were borrowed by later authors, including Chaucer and Shakespeare, just as he himself had borrowed and further developed some of them from ancient and medieval sources. He mastered Greek, studying Greek classics in the original language, and wrote scholarly Latin works on Greek mythology and geography. He helped to introduce the study of the Greek language and Greek literature at the University of Florence. Although he frequently attacked corrupt practices of the Church, he bequeathed his library to a priest and convent in Florence.

Like Petrarch, Boccaccio engaged enthusiastically in the task of collecting and editing classical works, an interest which became so widespread in Europe that numerous scholars devoted themselves to searching for ancient manuscripts in the monasteries. The study of Greek was revived in the West, and Greek scholars came from the East to meet the brisk demand for their instruction and books. Among them was the noted Greek scholar Manuel Chrysolores (1350–1415), who taught at the University of Florence in the late 1390s as the first professor of Greek and author of the first Greek grammar used in western Europe. He was followed by a long succession of Greek scholars who arrived in Italy during the fifteenth century, including refugees who fled Constantinople after the conquest of that city by the Turks in 1453.

EARLY HUMANIST EDUCATORS

Greek literature, ideals, and culture became a dominant educational interest of the Italian people, fostered by kings and wealthy citizens, especially Cosimo de' Medici (1393–1464), ruler of Florence, and his grandson Lorenzo the Magnificent (1449–1492), both of whom were patrons of art and literature, particularly Latin and Greek literature, and sponsored the collection and copying of ancient manuscripts. Aided by the wealthy Cosimo de' Medici, Pope Nicholas V (ca. 1397–1455) initiated the Vatican library; later in the fifteenth century, Rome became the leading European center of classical learning and culture.

The humanist spirit, given its greatest impetus by Petrarch and Boccaccio, soon inspired scholars throughout the Western world. Humanist studies in literature, art, and history spread among scholars and students at universities in Italy, France, Spain, Germany, and England, eventually influencing the curricula of Harvard and other colleges in the United States.

Humanists in Italy. In Italy, which contributed the first great humanists, Petrarch and Boccaccio, other eminent humanist scholars and educators included Poggio Bracciolini (1380–1459), papal secretary and discoverer of numerous lost classical works; Francesco Filfelfo (1398–1481), who taught girls as well as boys Hebrew literature and Greek classics in Florence and inspired the humanist views of Pope Pius II (Enea Silvio Piccolomini, 1405–1464), himself a gifted poet, historian, and geographer whose ideas on geography (like those of Roger Bacon in the thirteenth century) influenced Columbus; the Platonist philosopher Marsilio Ficino (1433–1499), who refused to accept Aristotle as the authority on everything but preferred Plato and wrote *Outlines of Platonic Thought,* emphasizing the need for love and brotherhood; and Pico della Mirandola (1463–1494), censured by the Church for his liberal views, a student of Hebrew, Arabic, mathematics, and philosophy, who agitated for education based on the ideals of various religions and the Greek and Roman classics. The Florentine Dominican prior Savonarola (1452–1498) fought the corruption of secular rulers and clergy, delivered sermons against Church authority, and condemned Alexander VI, the Borgia pope. Savonarola, whose views influenced many humanists, including Colet of England, was excommunicated in 1487, then tortured, hanged, and burned for heresy.

Humanists in France. In France François Villon (ca. 1431–1480), who studied at the University of Paris and later fell in with a band of thieves and was himself imprisoned for theft and murder, wrote emotional lyric poems about the common people, their pleasures, misfortunes, and sad fate, becoming one of the greatest French poets; Lefèvre d'Étaples (ca. 1450–1537), humanist leader and biblical scholar, condemned for heresy but later protected by the queen of Navarre, wrote liberal tracts on theological subjects and translated the Bible into French; and Guillaume Budé (or Budaeus, 1468–1540), royal librarian at Fontainebleu and a founder of the Collège de France, the foremost scholar in that country, initiated methods of research in the history of coinage and propagandized in behalf of classical learning and literature.

Humanists in Spain. In Spain the unidentified authors of the dramatized novel *Celestina* (1499) and the picaresque novel *Lazarillo di Tormes* (first published in Burgos, 1554) depicted the corrupt clergy in the Castilian dialect; and the humanist author Nebrija (or Nebrissensis, 1444–1532) wrote a Latin-Spanish dictionary and introduced the study of the Greek language and Greek literature at Seville and other centers of higher learning.

Humanists in Germany. In Germany the "Brethren of the Common Life," founded in Holland by the itinerant preacher Gerhard Groote (1340–1384), established numerous secondary schools teaching the common people Hebrew, Greek, Latin, and classical literature, and trained teachers of these subjects in many German high schools; Rudolph Agricola (1443–1485), a noted Dutch scholar, taught the classics in these schools and at Heidelberg University, which became a center of humanist education; and Johann Reuchlin (1455–1522), who had studied for a decade in Italy, taught Hebrew at Heidelberg University and wrote a Hebrew grammar. These scholars were soon followed by the Dutch humanist Desiderius Erasmus (ca. 1466–1536), who taught Greek at Cambridge University (England) and wrote Latin works, such as his highly popular *Encomium Moriae* (*Praise of Folly,* 1509), which contained satirical comments on the superstitions of the common people and the obsolete thinking and customs of the medieval Church, and his *Colloquies* (1526), denouncing absurd rituals, immoral Church practices, and public and private impostors. Erasmus wrote a Latin translation of the New Testament, including commentaries attacking the corruption and abuses of the Church, although he was a devout Christian and a moderate critic opposed to rebels or extremists. He advocated the teaching of geography, history, science, and good citizenship, with emphasis on the classics and ideals devoid of elaborate ceremonials. In treatises on education he stressed the need for moral and classical education of the multitude and elaborated on pedagogical principles, such as respect for individual differences of pupils, reminiscent of the ideas of Quintilian, whose works he studied and enthusiastically approved.

Humanists in England. In England Chaucer (ca. 1340–1400), the foremost poet of his time, wrote *The Canterbury Tales* and other works depicting all classes of people in typical life situations, borrowing some themes from Dante, Petrarch, and Boccaccio; William Langland (ca. 1332–1400), in his long poem, *Piers Plowman,* exposed widespread corruption in English society; William Grocyn (1446–1514) and Thomas Linacre (ca. 1460–1524), students of Greek language and literature, helped to establish classical learning at Oxford University; John Colet (ca. 1467–1519), who had studied law and Greek in France and Italy, and had been influenced, especially in Italy by Savonarola, to condemn Scholastic teachings, lectured on Saint Paul's Epistles and in 1510 founded Saint Paul's School as a secular humanist secondary school; and the humanist William Lily (1468–1533), headmaster of Saint Paul's school, wrote his popular *Latin Grammar* used in three hundred or more grammar schools of

England and later in New England schools. Sir Thomas More (1478–1535) in 1516 wrote in Latin his *Utopia,* which exposed the wretched condition of English society and painted an ideal community run on an altruistic and cooperative basis. (More, a loyal Catholic though he criticized clerical abuses, was beheaded by order of King Henry VIII for refusing to condemn papal authority or defend the king's divorce from Catherine of Aragon.) The diplomat and scholar Sir Thomas Elyot (ca. 1490–1546), a humanist friend of More's, wrote a treatise on the education of rulers, *The Governor,* concluding that secular officials should replace the clergy and wealthy favorites or interests in control over education and society. Roger Ascham (1515–1568), who taught Greek at Cambridge University and was a tutor of Queen Elizabeth, advocated the teaching of school subjects in the English language, humane treatment of pupils, and improved, practical methods of language instruction. He did not approve of travel on the Continent or experience as a means of learning, for they produce, he said, sophisticated manners or glib and clever, immoral or deceitful habits, and he insisted that reading a book is a necessary short cut to learning far preferable to experience.

Humanists as Moderate Reformers. Humanist authors, scholars, and educators in the major European countries during the fourteenth, fifteenth, and early sixteenth centuries spread the message and spirit of the new learning throughout the Western world, and their works became increasingly known and influential after the invention of movable printing type (about 1455), which made classical and contemporary writings widely available to students, scholars, and the common people. The humanists, for the most part, were not revolutionaries but rather moderate idealists interested in reforming the Church and redirecting education so that it would attend to the business of life on earth instead of only preparing people for the other world envisioned by Catholic Scholastics.

The humanist curriculum was adequate to prepare students for work in churches and schools and for advanced or specialized study of law and medicine. But it emphasized chiefly classical (Greek and Latin) literature and grammar, reading, writing, declamation and oratory, ancient history, mathematics, moral lessons, games and sports, music and dancing. (Music education was minimized in English schools, but excellent musical training was provided in German schools.) Gradually, however, the humanist, liberal approach to learning, which had replaced rigid Scholastic methods, deteriorated into drill work, narrow, formal analysis and memorization of subject matter, and a strict disciplinary form of instruction contrary to the original humanist spirit, which had stressed broad ideals and cultural values and attainments of the individual.

VITTORINO DA FELTRE

Humanist education in Italy during the fifteenth century, inspired initially by the work of Petrarch and Boccaccio, received the support of Italian ruling families, especially the Medicis in Florence, the Sforzas in Milan, the Estes in Ferrara and Milan, and the Gonzagas in Mantua. Wealthy families of the nobility became patrons of humanist court schools in which their sons and daughters could receive the best possible training in mind, body, and character. The interrelationships among these noble families were intricate, owing to numerous intermarriages. Many of their heads, decade after decade, were humanists and patrons of the arts, literature, and education.

The educator Vittorino da Feltre (1378–1446) taught private pupils in Padua and Venice, then lectured at the University of Padua, acquiring a fine reputation as a scholar and teacher. He became a tutor of children in the Gonzaga family and in 1423, with their cooperation, organized the famous "court school" at Mantua, where he conducted classes along humanist lines until his death in 1446.

Employing some of his former Venetian pupils as teachers, he assigned them to teach special subjects within their competence. He obtained commitments that there was to be no governmental regulation of, or interference with, the teachers. The pupils were mainly sons of the nobility, ages ten to twenty years, but he enrolled quite a few poor boys from the lower classes and saw to it that all pupils were treated on an equal footing. They boarded in the school and had their own student government.

Vittorino implemented the educational ideas of Quintilian in this school. The course of study centered on Greek and Latin language and literature, with emphasis upon reading, writing, and speaking both languages (using as models the poetry of Homer, Vergil, and Ovid, the orations of Demosthenes and Cicero, and other classics) and mastery of ancient history expounded in the works of Xenophon and Herodotus. Classical works were read and analyzed as wholes, not in bits and pieces. Subjects included geography, mathematics, art appreciation, music, morality, Christian ethics, and sports and games, in addition to grammar, language, history, and literature. Frequently the pace of instruction and the selection of subject matter were adjusted in the light of the interests and learning capacities of the pupils. Individual differences and the familiar activities of children in each age group became decisive factors affecting classroom instruction. Teachers in the school became so proficient in their methods of teaching that they were respected as almost the equals of university professors. In fact, the effective organization of subject matter and the superior methods of teaching in this school were adopted by other European schools and even impelled some of the universities to improve their own curricula and lectures.

GUARINO DA VERONA

The Italian humanist scholar Guarino da Verona (1370–1460) studied Greek in Constantinople and later acquired a wide reputation as a teacher of Greek classics to university students and as the editor of authoritative editions of Livy's *Annals of the Roman People,* Pliny the Elder's *Natural History,* and other works of classical literature. Like Vittorino da Feltre, he was greatly influenced by Quintilian's ideas on education, and he implemented many of Quintilian's proposals.

In 1429, aided by the family of Nicholas Este III (1384–1441), he organized a humanist school at Ferrara, which rivaled Vittorini's Mantuan school in fame and prestige, educating the children of some of the chief ruling Italian families. Typical products of this humanist schooling were two sisters in the Este family: Beatrice d'Este (1475–1497), duchess of Milan and the wife of Lodovico Sforza (duke of Bari), a beautiful princess who was a patron and friend of great artists, including Leonardo da Vinci; and Isabella d'Este (1474–1539), marchioness of Mantua (wife of the marquis Giovanni Francesco II Gonzaga), who employed renowned artists, including Raphael and Giulio Romano. Both sisters were skilled diplomats. Beatrice participated effectively in peace negotiations between Charles VIII of France and Italian royalty, while Isabella negotiated cleverly in her dealings with the cruel, unscrupulous Cesare Borgia, duke of Romagna.

The kind of classical education provided by these humanist schools of Vittorino da Feltre and Guarino da Verona resembled the programs of modern boarding schools for children in their teens, including competitive sports, guidance in health and morals, training in language expression, especially Latin declamation, and the study of history and ancient literature. On the secondary school level, the humanist design for education, inspired by ancient cultures, shaped instructional programs in Italy at the court schools, in southern France at the municipal colleges, in Holland and Germany at the schools of the "Brethren of the Common Life" and the Gymnasia, and in England and America at the grammar schools and later at the academies and preparatory schools. In higher education the humanist movement established the new learning during the fifteenth century in the universities of Italy (at Florence, Pavia, Rome, Milan, and Padua) under the leadership of famous classical scholars such as Barzizza (1370–1431) and Lorenzo Valla (1407–1457), then spread its influence to many other universities, including the universities of Paris, Heidelberg, Erfurt, Leipzig, Oxford, and Cambridge.

PART THREE — EDUCATORS IN MODERN TIMES

It will be recalled that the transition from ancient to medieval civilizations in the Western world during the first centuries of the Christian era resulted from long-term as well as immediate changes in society. The long-established social, political, and religious institutions and cultural patterns of the ancient world disappeared, displaced by new institutions and customs. Only a few ancient religious and ethical achievements, such as those of the Hebrews, persisted throughout medieval and modern periods, and for centuries the best intellectual and practical accomplishments of the ancient Greeks and Romans were either unknown or largely ignored.

The transition from medieval to modern times must also be attributed both to long-term and to immediate changes, but major medieval institutions and ideas survived as potent influences in human society. Ironically, it was the resurrection of ancient literature, culture, and educational aims in the thirteenth, fourteenth, and fifteenth centuries that speeded the process of institutional and cultural changes responsible for the new transition. Long-term causes of the evolution from medieval to modern civilization were European geographical and political expansion, the decline of feudalism and the guild system, the rise of national states, the commercial revolution and the development of capitalism, and the culture of the Renaissance initiated in Italy and later including the revival of science.

In Europe during the late fifteenth and early sixteenth centuries so many decisive immediate causes of social and cultural change occurred (within a few decades) that historians usually identify that period as marking the beginnings of modern times.

Two of the most significant developments were: (1) geographical explorations, from Columbus's voyages and discovery of America in 1492 to the circumnavigation of the earth by Magellan's ships in 1519; and (2) the Protestant revolt against the Roman Catholic Church, brought to a head by Martin Luther's defiance of papal authority in 1517. Of immense immediate influence, too, was the formation of new European monarchies and national states, particularly England and France and, later, Spain and Germany. The most important changes resulted from the ideas and works of famous scholars, artists, writers, scientists, and educators, especially the humanists and reformers (from Roger Bacon to Martin Luther) whose labors became the foundations of modern civilization.

JOHANNES STURM

The secondary schools and Church schools of Germany late in the fifteenth century changed their medieval type of curricula by introducing Greek and Latin language and classical literature, Hebrew, oratory, mathematics, and history. These schools became humanist in a narrow sense (more formal and disciplinary than the Italian schools of Vittorino da Feltre and Guarino da Verona), and many of them prospered throughout modern times. (Some failed because they did not provide the practical training needed for work in the commercial ventures of the busy towns.) A model school of this narrow humanist type, the Gymnasium at Strassburg, was established in 1537 by the famous educator Johannes Sturm (1507–1589), who had studied at Louvain University in Belgium, had taught in Paris, and had become well known as a teacher in the humanist schools of the "Brethren of the Common Life."

Sturm organized and closely supervised the instructional program of this Gymnasium. He divided the program into ten years or grades, with one teacher assigned to each grade and pupils classified according to age and academic progress. The general aims of his school were to mold the moral character of pupils to comport with Christian ethics, to develop their proficiency in self-expression, especially in speaking and writing Latin, and to make certain that they mastered thoroughly the specific facts and elements of each subject in the curriculum. Sturm provided for systematic practice and drill work in language usage, writing, declaiming, and dramatization, giving examinations to ascertain achievement and providing immediate correction of errors. Latin was the sole language of everyday classroom conversation between teachers and pupils. The Latin language and Latin classics were studied all ten years of the program, and Latin, not German, was the language used in the five-year course of study of Greek language and literature. Physical education was neglected. Science, mathematics, and history were excluded from the curriculum. There was no time for lessons in personal manners or conduct; good behavior and strict attention to the business of learning were simply required and expected. Pupils were kept busy with systematic drill or exercises and required reading, writing, conversation, question-answer quizzes, declamations, and recitations.

Sturm explained his educational program in two widely read pedagogical treatises: *Plan of Organization* (1538) and *Letters to the Masters* (1565). Teachers in many European countries admired and adopted his plan of school organization, his curriculum, and his teaching methods. The educational aims and policies he popularized during four decades of service as head of the Strassburg Gymnasium became permanent features in the schools of Germany. As late as 1843 the famous American educator Horace Mann, reporting on German schools then administered by the central government, praised the graded system of instruction; practice and drill in reading, writing, and speech; emphasis on classical studies and Christian ethics; and the insistence by teachers that pupils correct mistakes promptly, give complete answers to specific questions, and speak correctly—in other words, the identical standards of mastery and perfection prescribed by Johannes Sturm in the sixteenth century.

MARTIN LUTHER

The broad humanist ideas of Erasmus and the narrower humanist educational program of Sturm did not reject, but in fact emphasized respect for, the teachings of the Christian Church. None of the leading humanists were theological cynics or violent revolutionaries. The Waldenses, Albigenses, Wycliffites, and Hussites sincerely opposed corrupt activities of the clergy and arbitrary authority (from their point of view), but all were pious devotees of the Bible. John Huss, defiantly rejecting papal edicts he believed to be contrary to the will of God, committed his soul to Christ and prayed constantly while the flames were burning him at the stake. Such dissenters had little or no chance of achieving Church reforms through their campaigns. Even the moderate Erasmus, who wrote eloquently about the follies of Church officials, and stressed the necessity for living a virtuous Christian life, but avoided taking sides in violent controversies, found his books banned at the University of Paris and later at all Catholic schools.

Nonetheless the constant demands for reform of the Church, the spreading discontent, and the papal schisms had a cumulative effect that impelled the Council of Constance (1514) to propose changes in Church government designed to correct abuses by the clergy and even to democratize Church affairs. Unfortunately, the proposals were never implemented. The old authoritative policies remained in effect and were in fact strengthened. The stage was set for a new wave of dissension, especially among the German people, who deeply resented the use of their taxes and contributions for enterprises of little or no value to them, including projects of corrupt Italian Church officials appointed by the pope to high positions in the German Church. During this critical period Martin Luther (1483–1546) became the leader of the discontented German noblemen and common people.

Life and Works of Martin Luther.   Martin Luther was born in 1483 at Eisleben, a town near Leipzig in northwestern Saxony. His father Hans, a Thuringian peasant, leased and worked several furnaces in the mines of nearby Mansfield, settled there, and became a respected member of the village council. It was his hope that Martin would study law. The boy attended a local school and also the school of the "Brethren of the Common Life" in Magdeburg. In 1501 he enrolled at the University of Erfurt, which was then under the influence of the Nominalist philosophy of William of Ockham and employed some humanist faculty members. He was a diligent student of Latin classics and Christian theology, a skilled musician, and popular among fellow students. Suddenly, after receiving his bachelor's and master's degrees, Martin entered the Erfurt Convent of the Augustinian order to become a friar. In 1508 he worked as a preacher to the monks of Wittenberg, subsequently returning to Erfurt University, where he earned the advanced degree of Doctor of Holy Scripture. Soon thereafter he was appointed professor of theology at Wittenberg University by the Elector of Saxony, Frederick III (the Wise) (1463–1525), founder (in 1502) of that university.

Luther's ideas about Scholasticism were based on Ockham's Nominalist position as interpreted by the German philosopher Gabriel Biel 1403–1495), who wrote influential works, such as the *Epitome and Collection from Ockham* and *On the Power and Use of Money*. Luther agreed with Biel about the need for each human being to find for and by himself the true path to salvation. He insisted upon the futility of good works and Church rituals for this purpose, and he concluded that only faith, not indulgences or any other payments or external influences devised by the Church hierarchy, could save anyone's soul from the consequences of sin. He declared that neither human reason nor Aristotelian logic, and no Scholastic theory or practice, could serve as a means of redemption. He put his own faith in the efficacy of faith itself, in the power of intuitive, mystical faith to communicate with the divine Presence and receive salvation directly by the grace of God.

The sale of indulgences by agents of the Church had degenerated into a revenue-producing procedure, a lucrative source of income for the pope's treasury. In ancient times when members of a Christian congregation confessed their sins, they did so in public and promised to perform good deeds as proof of sincere repentance. In Luther's time individuals confessed their sins in private to a priest and often could easily obtain absolution from the Church by purchasing indulgences from a papal agent even though they did not actually repent or do anything else as a penance except pay for their purchase. They could sin, pay, and forget, ready to repeat. In 1517 when a sales agent, the monk

John Tetzel, appeared in localities near Saxony to sell an indulgence decreed by the pope, Frederick III refused to admit him. (The pope, Leo X, of the Medici family, was a patron of the arts and needed funds for the work by Michelangelo on Saint Peter's Cathedral in Rome.) Many people hurried out of Wittenberg to purchase the indulgence tickets. Luther denounced these transactions and displayed his views to the public by nailing ninety-five theses about indulgences on the local church door. His theses, translated promptly from Latin into German, aroused intense interest and emotional reactions among university students and the common people. The University of Wittenberg Press printed thousands of copies, which were distributed so widely that the sale of indulgences quickly declined.

The pope issued a summons against Luther but withdrew it after the University of Wittenberg and Frederick III objected that it would injure the university. A continuing lively debate followed between papal supporters and Luther, who studied the situation further, only to discover that widespread fraud and deceit were involved in the sale of indulgences. He then attacked a whole array of Church abuses, analyzing them in public, and finally asserted that the Church had made a grave error in condemning the martyr John Huss. In 1520 he wrote three pamphlets to explain his views, not only denouncing the fraudulent indulgences and other corrupt practices but also rejecting the authority of the Church to interpose itself between individual worshipers and their God. He demanded reforms both in the doctrines and in the practices of the hierarchy. Christians had no need, Luther wrote, for any institution or intermediaries to tell them what to believe or do, no need for anything except the Bible and their faith in God.

The Pope issued a bull in 1520 excommunicating Luther, who promptly burned the document at the university in the presence of enthusiastic students. The newly crowned Holy Roman Emperor Charles V, a loyal Catholic, thereupon summoned Luther to defend himself at the Diet of Worms in 1521. Luther made a vigorous defense but was banned from the empire as a first step toward his elimination. Immediately, however, his friends hurried him secretly to a place of refuge, the castle of

Frederick III in Wartburg. He remained there two years writing a notable pamphlet about monastic vows and completing his famous translation of the New Testament from Hebrew and Greek texts into modern German.

Luther did not believe in social revolution. He favored gradual reforms of society by religious and secular leaders. He had no confidence in democratic political action or in the judgment of the masses concerning social issues, and he rejected violence as a means of reform. Although in 1520 he had urged the German princes to rebel against the Church if it refused to correct its abuses, he desired only an opportunity for individuals to return to the basic beliefs found in the Bible and the writings of Saint Augustine. When the German peasants refused to await a gradual improvement in their living conditions and revolted in 1524, issuing their demands in *Twelve Articles,* Luther denounced them and declared that they should be repressed by the German princes, as indeed, they were; many peasants blamed him for the consequences.

The break with the Roman Catholic Church about religious doctrines and practices could not, however, be compromised. The continued religious controversies stimulated dissatisfaction against established authority in political and social as well as religious institutions. As Luther's protests and proposed reforms spread throughout northern Europe, quarrels broke out between princes or kings and popes (for example, between Charles V and Pope Clement VII). Wars between nations erupted in a confusing struggle for power. Religious wars between Roman Catholics and Lutherans began in 1522 when Franz von Sickingen's league of Lutherans was defeated by the combined forces of the archbishop of Trier (Treves) and various German princes, and such wars continued long after Luther's death in 1546, making the split in the Christian Church permanent. Lutheranism soon dominated in northern and western Germany, Denmark, Sweden, Norway, and some towns in Lithuania and Hungary.

Luther's most influential writings were his three pamphlets of 1520 on theological doctrines, in which he called Pope Leo X the most evil bandit in all past, present, and future times (entitled *On the Liberty of a Christian Man, An Address to the Christian*

Nobility of the German Nation, and *On the Babylonian Captivity of the Church of God*); his translation of the entire Bible into German (1522–1534), a clear and accurate work completed with the help of his colleagues Philipp Melanchthon and Johannes Bugenhagen and accepted throughout northern and western Europe by students and the common people; his letter of 1524, "To the Councilmen of All Towns in German Lands on Their Obligation to Send Children for Instruction in Christian Schools"; his treatise, *Augsburg Confession* (1530), summarizing the main tenets of the Lutheran faith; and his remarkable collection of thirty-seven hymns, including some of his own compositions. His translation of the Bible into German had a great influence on German society, religion, education, language, and literature, comparable to the influence of the King James Bible in English-speaking countries.

Luther's Ideas on Education.   Luther's religious beliefs shaped his philosophy of education. He insisted that the home and the family, as well as the church and the school, must provide essential elements of a good Christian educational program. He held that the home and the family are in fact the primary foundations of educational and social institutions, that, since all children are equally God's children, education should be universal, free, and compulsory, that parents should make certain that every child receives an education at home and in school so that he will become a good Christian citizen who will read, understand, and work and live in accordance with the Bible. It is the duty of the state, he declared, to provide funds for the support of education and to control the schools, compelling the attendance of children in order to realize the religious and civic aims of instruction. Religious doctrines, he said, should be compatible with all the educational objectives and programs of a religiously oriented state, thereby achieving a morally virtuous, militarily strong, and prosperous nation. Since there will be no need in such a plan to pay taxes to the Catholic Church, the government will be able to contribute adequate funds for education.

Luther believed that specific educational programs should include both school and home instruction for boys and girls alike. Children in primary schools, he urged, should attend classes in reading and writing German, in Bible study, and in school subjects, including music, history, arithmetic, nature study, and physical education; at home they should learn practical skills required for a trade or homemaking. Latin secondary schools should teach Latin, Greek, Hebrew, rhetoric, history, mathematics and science, logical argumentation, music, gymnastics, and sports (fencing and wrestling), for all these subjects are necessary, he asserted, in order to prepare students for the obligations of citizenship, for religious life, and for advanced studies. (Luther, himself a composer of hymns, stressed the importance of musical education, especially singing and choral music for church services. Music became a prominent subject in German schools.)

According to Luther, the universities should provide instruction to prepare students for the professions of theology, law, and medicine and for positions in the churches and the state, but they should eliminate the study of Church canon law, as well as most of Greek science and philosophy, and should study the Bible instead of Peter Lombard's twelfth-century textbook (the *Book of Sentences*) used in Roman Catholic universities. All teachers in schools should be trained for their occupation, and clergymen should also receive adequate training and experience in teaching. Instruction to meet the practical needs of the community should be combined with the study of the Scriptures. Luther condemned reliance upon reason and experimentation as a method of discovering truth, and he denounced the ideas of Copernicus (1473–1543), the founder of modern astronomy, whose work was anathema both to pious Catholics and to Protestants who refused to believe that the earth is not the center of the universe.

Luther advocated a method of learning through constant practice with concepts and skills, stressing logical reasoning and the ideas (not the literary style) of the works. He also approved of insistence by teachers upon correct language usage and the study of grammar. He condemned the superstitions widespread among the common people, particularly their trust in astrology (although he himself believed in dreams and miracles), and he declared that religion must be a core ingredient of school lessons. Teachers, he said, should keep in mind the preparation of children for good citizenship, the development of religious character, and the well-being of society as a whole, rejecting the narrow rituals and indoctrination emphasized by the monks in Catholic schools.

Luther's ideas and Lutheran churches and schools spread rapidly. He succeeded in popularizing the same theological point of view enunciated in vain by numerous predecessors, including, for example, the Italian martyr Savonarola and the Bohemian martyr Huss. Luther had certain decisive advantages, especially the printing press to disseminate his views widely, the steady growth of German nationalism, the backing of German rulers eager to eliminate Church taxes, and support by prosperous merchants who welcomed a new theological approach that would justify and protect instead of condemning or consuming the profits of their business enterprises. Changing commercial, political, technological, and social conditions explain why, after Savonarola and Huss had failed in the fifteenth century, Luther finally succeeded in the sixteenth century.

THREE PROTESTANT EDUCATORS

The general principles of education expounded by Luther were implemented by highly competent school administrators and educators, especially Philipp Melanchthon (1497–1560) and Johannes Bugenhagen (1485–1558) in Germany; and similar ideas were also popularized by the humanist reformer Huldreich Zwingli (1484–1531) in Switzerland.

Melanchthon, a colleague of Luther at the University of Wittenberg, collaborated with him in his translation of the Bible and succeeded in implementing Lutheran ideas at the university. Thousands of trained teachers streamed from the University of Wittenberg into other universities and the Latin secondary schools and Gymnasia throughout southern and central regions of Germany, disseminating the new faith and learning. He was a prolific writer whose numerous works became standard textbooks in the study of Greek and Latin, history, argumentation, ethics, and theology. Of greatest importance was his survey of German schools, reported in his *Book of Visitation* (1528), a pioneering investigation that cleared the way for the later establishment of centralized school systems on a statewide or national basis. In 1528 Saxony adopted a plan for church and school reorganization prepared by Melanchthon. Within several decades the public schools of Germany implemented his plan, modified in some respects, providing instruction for girls as well as boys and requiring compulsory attendance, even to the extent of imposing fines on parents who kept their children out of school. Eventually, after the Thirty Years' War (1618–1648) and the Treaty of Westphalia (which confirmed the sovereignty of the various nations of Europe), the school system of Prussia further improved upon Melanchthon's original plans, and the new learning became dominant in German schools throughout the eighteenth and nineteenth centuries. (Nineteenth-century modifications increased the degree of centralization of schools and largely eliminated theological influence and control.)

While Philipp Melanchthon was reorganizing schools and churches in southern and central Germany, his humanist colleague at Wittenberg University, Johannes Bugenhagen, was performing the same service for towns in northern Germany. Bugenhagen was a Pomeranian priest, rector, and lecturer on the Bible at religious schools when Luther's writing inspired him with enthusiasm for Lutheran theological views. He joined the faculty at Wittenberg University in 1521, earning a wide reputation for eloquence and administrative ability. Beginning in 1528 he devoted his time to revamping the churches and schools in towns such as Brunswick, Hamburg, and Lübeck, as well as in Pomerania and Schleswig-Holstein, establishing parish schools in which girls and boys could learn to read and write German and study the Bible. So many of the schools adopted his curriculum and teaching methods that he became known as the father of the German system of schools (the *Volksschule*) for the common people.

In Denmark the brutal king Christian II had been driven out of the country in 1523, and his able successor, King Christian III (1503–1559), known as the father of his country, invited Bugenhagen to undertake the reorganization of Danish religious and educational institutions. During several years in Denmark,

Bugenhagen succeeded in converting the University of Copenhagen as well as numerous Danish churches and schools into Lutheran centers. He then returned to Wittenberg to continue his scholarly research and writing until his death in 1558. Among his published works are a history of his native state of Pomerania and various theological treatises, including *Interpretation of the Book of Psalms* (1523).

Also inspired by Luther's views, Ulrich (or Huldreich) Zwingli, a priest in Zurich who was an admirer of Erasmus's humanist ideas, advocated the return to the faith of the Gospels and became a popular exponent of the new learning. In his *Commentary on the True and False Religion* (1525) he expounded Luther's doctrines, objected to some of them, and split the dissenters into competing groups. In his sermons and writings on the Christian education of children, he advocated the establishment of numerous elementary schools for the teaching of humanist studies. He was far more democratic than Luther in regard to political and social issues; moreover, his advocacy of popular self-government won for him broad support in the Swiss cantons of Zurich and Bern. The Council of Zurich defended him in doctrinal quarrels with Pope Adrian VI (1459–1523). The councilors were not only amenable to his theological views but also grateful for his espousal of equal voting rights for Zurich at a time when the opposing cantons had disproportionate voting power. Unfortunately, the Protestants at a conference between Zwingli and Luther at Marburg in 1529 failed to agree on a compromise and remained divided. In 1531, during a civil war between Catholic and Protestant cantons, Zwingli was killed, his body mutilated and burned by Catholic soldiers. During Zwingli's lifetime he had seen put into effect his demand that the civil government control Church, school, and state institutions. Owing chiefly to his efforts, the population of Switzerland divided almost equally between Catholics and Protestants, and it has so remained to this day.

JOHN CALVIN

During Luther's time the French Protestant reformer, theologian, and educator John Calvin (1509–1564) accepted many

Lutheran doctrines, such as pure faith in the Bible, but rejected others, including the Lutheran belief in the actual presence of Christ's body and blood in the sacrament of the Lord's Supper. He emphasized especially the universality of sin in every human being at birth.

Career of John Calvin.   In his own career Calvin shifted about from theological and philosophical Scholastic studies in Parisian colleges and service as a Catholic chaplain, curate, and preacher to the study of law at Orléans University (1528), where he lectured occasionally on law and also studied classical and humanist literature, becoming highly sympathetic to Protestantism before moving to Bourges in 1529. Subsequently, at the University of Paris, he learned to read Greek and Hebrew and wrote a treatise in Latin about one of Seneca's works (1532). He taught the Lutheran doctrine of salvation through faith and in 1533 assisted the rector of the university in defending that doctrine, narrowly escaping arrest for his efforts. The following year Calvin gave up his Catholic posts as chaplain and curate in order to oppose the Catholic Church, whereupon he was arrested and (briefly) twice imprisoned. Now a staunch Protestant, he fled to Strassburg and then to Basel, where in 1536 he published anonymously his famous *Institutes of the Christian Religion* in Latin, later translating portions of the volume into French in order to publicize Protestant beliefs.

Settled eventually in Geneva, Calvin became a popular religious, political, and educational leader. The church, he insisted, should be in control of education and public morals, as well as religious doctrines and practices. His views were adopted by the Geneva government which eliminated Catholic worship, prohibited heretical writings, and decreed that all persons should work hard, avoiding the sin of idleness, live humbly and frugally, obey the laws, reject any form of luxury or amusement, and devote themselves to faith and prayer. Principles of private property, business profits, interest on loans, and support of trade were regarded as justifiable, but individuals were expected to be ever ready to sacrifice selfish advantage for sake of the commonweal.

Views and Influence of Calvin.   Calvin was just as intolerant as the Roman Catholic hierarchy whom he had condemned for their intolerance and persecution of dissenters. When the Spanish theologian Servetus (1511–1553) opposed traditional Catholic beliefs in the Trinity and also the baptism of infants, he was charged with heresy by the Inquisition; when he escaped to Geneva, Calvin had him imprisoned and burned at the stake as a heretic, an action approved by the Catholic Church and by Luther's colleague and friend Philipp Melanchthon.

Calvin represented a most rigorous form of Protestantism, one requiring strict obedience to Church and state, self-discipline, and pure faith in God's omnipotent will, upon which all born sinners and their fate depend. Calvinism was adopted by the Huguenots in France, the Presbyterians in Scotland, the Reformed Dutch in Holland, and the Puritans in England. In the latter country the Anglicans represented to some extent a compromise between Protestant and Roman Catholic theological views. In the American colonies Calvinist ideas in behalf of free public education based upon religious ideals inspired citizens of Massachusetts to organize town schools during the seventeenth century.

Calvin's ideas on education, to which he devoted much attention in his later years, stressed civic training and strict discipline based on moral teachings and the study of school subjects, including the native language, the Bible, arithmetic, reading in French, Latin, and Greek, rhetoric, logic, elocution, and music; the provision of primary, secondary (collegiate), and higher education on an equal footing for all classes of the population, supported and controlled by the Church and aided by funds of the towns; the appointment of educated schoolmasters by Church authorities; and the training of Protestant leaders for every phase of the political, social, religious, educational, and economic life of the community.

Calvin's disciple, the noted statesman and religious radical reformer John Knox (1505–1572), wrote numerous influential treatises to disseminate Calvinist ideas in Scotland. The Protestant churches of Scotland eventually assumed control of the parish schools and the national educational system, a policy

Calvin and Knox recommended. The activities of Knox and his followers helped the English Protestants to defeat the Catholics of Mary, Queen of Scots (Mary Stuart, 1542–1587), whom Knox compared to Jezebel, the biblical Phoenician princess who was responsible for the persecution of Hebrew prophets and the murder of the vineyard owner Naboth. Having been deposed by the Scots, Mary fled to England, where she was imprisoned and in 1587 beheaded for treason in accordance with the instructions of Queen Elizabeth, who had herself been excommunicated in 1570 by Pope Pius V.

The ideas of Calvin and Knox in favor of Church control over education had a lasting influence upon the schools of many countries. Luther had recommended the contrary policy of control by civil government. In democratic nations the trend eventually brought separation between Church and state, a principle which a radical segment of Protestantism in England had vainly tried to introduce. Even in democratic countries, however, with populations divided into numerous competing sects, religious leaders and religious ideals continued to influence educational aims and practices. Nevertheless, the destruction of the Church monopoly in Europe made it possible for the new learning to spread and cleared a path for scientific methods in education and society.

IGNATIUS LOYOLA

Ignatius Loyola (1491–1556) was born into a family of the Spanish nobility at Loyola, Guipúzcoa. He became a soldier, Church leader, educator, and founder of the Society of Jesus, the Jesuit order approved by Pope Paul III in 1540.

Life and Works of Loyola. Loyola kept diaries relating the details of his remarkable career—how in his youth he had lived a dissolute life, had served as an uneducated soldier until he was severely wounded in the legs, underwent painful surgery but remained partly crippled, and while recovering from his ordeal studied religious treatises that convinced him he should devote himself to the service of the Catholic Church.

At the age of thirty-three, Loyola attended an elementary school to learn how to read and write; later he studied at several universities, including the University of Paris, which had banned the writings of both Erasmus and Luther. For a time he resided at the home in Bruges of the noted Spanish humanist philosopher Juan Luis Vives (1492–1541), an opponent of Scholasticism who favored inductive methods of scientific research and taught philosophy at Oxford University until obliged to leave when he refused to approve the divorce of Henry VIII from Catherine of Aragon.

In 1537 Loyola was ordained to the priesthood. After suffering numerous adversities, including several arrests by the Inquisition for alleged deviations in belief or conduct, he planned and with several friends founded the association of Jesuits, of which he was elected general in 1541.

The Jesuits.   The Jesuit Society was designed to help stem the Protestant tide in religion, politics, and education. The primary aim was to restore or reinforce the faith, works, and authority of the Catholic Church in European lands with newly enlarged Protestant minorities and those recently brought under Protestant domination. The order contributed greatly to the successful efforts of the hierarchy to retain the allegiance of the Catholic majorities in Italy, Spain, Portugal, France, Poland, Austria, Ireland, and other strongholds of the Roman Church, and also to win more adherents in Germany, Scandinavia, and England.

Loyola applied the lessons learned from his military experience to good advantage, insisting upon observance of the following principles: (1) strict discipline and obedience to the Church hierarchy; (2) use of good means for good ends, honest methods of achieving objectives of the Church; (3) training of faithful leaders by means of persuasion and education, prudently avoiding violent methods that might restrain a few potential critics but would create thousands of new enemies; and (4) uniformity in thoughts and decisions among all Catholics, with absolute exclusion of novel or questionable ideas in religion or education.

The Jesuits were eminently successful in their educational work. They combined the best practices of the Calvinist educators with the organizational plans of Sturm and, despite some doubts on Loyola's part, included many humanist studies in the curricula of their Latin secondary schools and universities. Latin and Greek, Ciceronian oratory, rhetoric, logic, philosophy, health education and sports, history, mathematics, science, and, of course, theology were emphasized. Students were required to master every topic in each subject thoroughly, and the methods of instruction featured detailed lectures and explanations by the teacher, class discussions, theme writing, drill and memorization through reviews at frequent intervals, competition among students for prizes, and debates and examinations, all directed closely by a highly selective, trained corps of teachers.

During the sixteenth and seventeenth centuries, the Jesuits contributed little to elementary education, a field the Church had neglected for a millennium. In Catholic countries, however, especially France and Italy, other teaching orders were encouraged by Jesuit accomplishments to train elementary school teachers for villages and towns, enabling children of the common people to learn the three Rs, the catechism, Latin grammar, and music.

In the Jesuit secondary schools and universities, all students were closely supervised by monitors, teachers, prefects, and rectors, a hierarchy that constantly checked and evaluated every phase of activity to make certain that the program conformed in practice to the plan of studies prescribed in minute detail by the order. The extreme formalism and strict theological control of educational tasks made it difficult to adjust them to new information and changing social and cultural conditions. During the eighteenth and nineteenth centuries the prestige of these schools declined as ideals of inductive scientific inquiry, individual initiative, and democratic self-direction became increasingly popular in Western education. Jesuit and other Church schools and universities lost ground steadily in the twentieth century because of burdensome costs and especially the development of national school systems, which established secular public schools, colleges, and universities.

Other Teaching Orders.   In addition to the Jesuits, various other teaching orders were founded during the sixteenth and seventeenth centuries in order to achieve on the elementary school level the same broad objectives of Catholic education as those of the Jesuit secondary schools. Some of the teaching orders became permanent centers of elementary education, serving multitudes of Catholic children in many Western countries. Among influential orders were the Order of the Ursulines (1535), the Sisters of Notre Dame (1598), the Piarists (1621), the Jansenists of Port Royal (1631), and the Brethren of the Christian Schools (1684).

The educational program of the Brethren of the Christian Schools was developed by Saint Jean Baptiste de la Salle (1651–1719). La Salle, the son of a wealthy French merchant, organized an initial elementary school in 1679 at Rheims and founded the Institute of the Brethren of the Christian Schools in 1684 at Rouen. He trained teachers for the Institute's numerous elementary schools established throughout France during the eighteenth century. Subsequently the Institute became very active in other West European countries and in the United States. These free schools enrolled boys and girls of the poor, teaching them basic primary school subjects (the three Rs) in their native tongue, as well as religious beliefs, morals, and good manners. A number of trade, technical, and academic secondary schools were also organized to supplement the elementary school programs.

Schools of the Christian Brethren emulated some features of Johannes Sturm's perfectionist philosophy of education, particularly his system of grades, class responses in recitations, frequent examinations, drill work, attention to and respect for the teacher, and strict discipline (even physical punishment being prescribed in accordance with fixed rules), contrasted with the generally harsh treatment of schoolchildren during the seventeenth and eighteenth centuries. La Salle organized a training school for the education of teachers, requiring practice teaching under supervision as a prominent part of the course of study. In many European countries the Institute's numerous schools provided free basic education for poor boys and girls guided by well-qualified elementary schoolteachers. In the same way the elementary schools of other Catholic teaching orders contributed to Church objectives, and some of the orders have survived to this day despite the dominance of free, secular, tax-supported public education in Western lands.

RICHARD MULCASTER

Richard Mulcaster (1530–1611), for twenty-five years the headmaster of the famous Merchant Taylors' School of London (supported by funds of craftsmen working with linen and other tailoring fabrics) and later a high master of Saint Paul's School (founded in 1510 by the humanist educator John Colet), formulated principles of education quite different from those advocated by the Jesuits. The principles expounded in Mulcaster's pedagogical treatise entitled *Positions* in 1581 were partially implemented in his grammar (secondary) schools but were not widely accepted elsewhere, for they were far in advance of his time, emphasizing the adaptation of teaching procedures to the interests and abilities of individual pupils; the development of good health and intellectual powers as a basic aim of education; the use of a well-rounded curriculum, including oral and instrumental music, art, and mastery of reading and writing English; exclusion of pressure or harsh discipline; provision of basic education in schools (not by tutors in the home) for all children; and the organization of teacher-training colleges to prepare prospective teachers for the profession.

Among the famous graduates of the Merchant Taylors' School during Mulcaster's directorship was the renowned poet Edmund Spenser (1552–1599), author of *The Faerie Queene* and other English classics. As a student in the school, Spenser studied Latin but concentrated on mastery of English, developing superb skill in poetry and translating selections from Petrarch's Latin into fine English verse. At graduation Spenser received scholarship funds from the estate of the London philanthropist Robert Nowell, which enabled him to enroll at Pembroke College of Cambridge University, with which Mulcaster's school had a close relationship.

Mulcaster did not oppose the Roman classics as an important segment of the curriculum, but he insisted on teaching all subjects in the English language, a feature adopted not only in

British grammar schools but also in America, where in the seventeenth century the Latin grammar schools began to prepare boys for college and university studies leading to careers in the ministry, law, and medicine. The pioneering Boston Latin Grammar School founded in 1635, the oldest public school in America—whose distinguished alumni have included Benjamin Franklin and Charles W. Eliot, for forty years president of Harvard University—has to this day reflected in many ways the aims and principles of education advocated by Mulcaster. He agreed with Roger Ascham that wide reading of books in the English language is far superior to travel or personal experience as a method of learning. Although he recommended universal education for all children of both sexes, he held that instruction should be geared to the needs and capacities of individual learners and that, therefore, advanced or specialized studies should be taught only to well-qualified pupils prepared to benefit from them. This principle differed markedly from the rigid, minutely prescribed curriculum of the Jesuit system. Mulcaster's conception is comparable to the principle of readiness for learning espoused by twentieth-century psychologists and educators. (According to this principle, a child who is well prepared for a learning task is likely to enjoy it and succeed, whereas one who is not well prepared is apt to dislike the assigned task and fail.)

EARLY MODERN SCIENTISTS, PHILOSOPHERS, AND WRITERS

In the fifteenth century progress in education emphasized mastery of literature and the arts. In the sixteenth century educators stressed the attainment of moral, religious, and social ideals through education. In the sixteenth and seventeenth centuries, pioneering scientists, philosophers, and writers built the principal intellectual foundations of modern civilization. These great thinkers represented many different countries, ethnic and linguistic backgrounds, and types of personality. They had in common a faith in the capacity of the human intellect to solve the most challenging problems in every field of endeavor. Each created new ways of thought and new methods destined to illuminate many aspects of the natural environment and to redirect to some extent human nature and conduct. Their ideas and works could not be restrained for long by static theological or political institutions; in fact, attempts at repression often merely increased their influence. By means of direct or indirect communication they benefited from one another's thoughts. They disseminated their new ideas through lectures and writings, professional societies, and educational institutions. They were great educators, for their ideas gradually permeated the books, language, and customs of all humanity, transforming individual and social life.

Early Modern Scientists. The most influential scientists of this period were *Nicolaus Copernicus* (1473–1543), the Polish astronomer and physician who rejected the ancient Ptolemaic theory that the earth is the center of the universe and inaugurated modern astronomy with his contrary theory that the earth rotates on its axis daily and the planets revolve around the sun; *Andreas Vesalius* (1514–1564), the Belgian anatomist (condemned by the Church for his dissection of the human body), who used the techniques of dissection and observation to analyze in great detail the structures of the human body and its parts, correcting numerous errors made by the ancient Greek physician Galen, and thus founded the science of modern anatomy; *William Gilbert* (1540–1603), the English experimental physicist (and physician to Queen Elizabeth) who founded the science of magnetism and electricity; *Galileo* (1564–1642), the Italian physicist who discovered fundamental laws of motion, such as the law of falling bodies, the path of a projectile, the satellites of Jupiter, and the sunspots, and also invented improved scientific instruments, such as the thermometer, refracting telescope, and hydrostatic balance; *Johannes Kepler* (1571–1630), the crippled German astronomer who traced and calculated the movements of the planets, identifying their elliptical paths, the effects of distance from the sun upon their rates of travel, and the law governing their revolutions—basic principles of physical astronomy; *William Harvey* (1578–1657), the English anatomist and physician who was the first to discover and publish the principal facts concerning blood circulation, postulating the circuits of the blood through the veins, the arteries, and the structures of the heart; *René Descartes* (1596–

1650), the French mathematician and philosopher who developed analytic geometry and graphic methods (and made decisive contributions to modern philosophy); *Robert Boyle* (1627–1691), the Irish chemist and physicist, a wealthy propagandist for the Christian religion, who became the founder of modern chemistry; *Marcello Malpighi* (1628–1694), the Italian physiologist and professor of medicine who pioneered in the use of microscopes to discover and describe many fine details about the structures and functions of plants and animals, including human blood corpuscles, lungs, glands, and brain; *Christian Huygens* (1629–1695), the Dutch physicist who invented the pendulum clock and discovered the laws of the pendulum and of inelastic bodies, making possible the development of modern dynamics; *Anton von Leeuwenhoek* (1632–1723), the Dutch naturalist who built microscopes and used them to isolate minute bodies, such as red blood corpuscles, spermatozoa, and bacteria; *Robert Hooke* (1635–1703), the English professor of mathematics at Oxford University and chemist who made discoveries about the nature of combustion, the rotation of Jupiter, light waves, the law of inverse squares, and the cell structure of plants; and, above all, *Isaac Newton* (1642–1727), the English physicist who proved the revolution of the planets around the sun and disclosed numerous laws and facts about gravitation, light, and color—new concepts and types of calculation basic to modern sciences, including mathematics, physics, optics, astronomy, and mechanics.

Early Modern Philosophers. The most influential philosophers were *Michel de Montaigne* (1533–1592), the French essayist and philosophical skeptic, a tolerant critic of human nature who advised men to accept natural events equably, adjusting themselves to nature, especially since their powers of interference are distinctly limited; *Francis Bacon* (1561–1626), the leading English philosopher of inductive science, dedicated to the collection of facts through experiments and observation as bases for unprejudiced conclusions; *Thomas Hobbes* (1588–1679), the English social, political, and scientific philosopher who believed that man is a physical organism, that in the natural state of mankind might makes right until each person agrees to accept a contract with society so that, if he obeys the laws imposed by the ruler or state, he will enjoy the advantages of living in a peaceful community; René Descartes (1596–1650), the French mathematician and philosopher, previously mentioned, who applied mathematical reasoning to philosophy, initiated new trends in metaphysics and epistemology based on his rule never to believe anything unless it can be proved by reasoning, and became an important founder of modern philosophy; *Benedict Spinoza* (1632–1677), the Portuguese Jewish leader of a pantheistic, monist school of philosophy asserting that all things are subject to a law of necessity and are uniformly spiritual or divine in their ultimate nature; *Gottfried Wilhelm Leibniz* (1646–1716), the German Rationalist philosopher and mathematician, creator of the calculus and concepts of symbolic logic, who refused to teach in any university because educational standards, he said, had sunk too low; and *John Locke* (1632–1704), the English physician and leader of the Empiricist school of philosophy, which stated that all knowledge is derived from sense experience and from ideas based on such experience.

Early Modern Writers. Among the most influential of early modern writers were *Desiderius Erasmus* (ca. 1466–1536), who wrote his works in Latin, including *The Praise of Folly,* the *Colloquies,* and his translation of the New Testament; *Martin Luther* (1483–1546), who wrote his works in German, including his theological treatises, various prose works, hymns, and translation of the Bible; and *John Calvin* (1509–1564), who wrote *The Institutes of the Christian Religion* in Latin and later translated the Latin version into masterly French. There were many great writers in the sixteenth and seventeenth centuries who wrote in their native languages.

Writers in Italian were *Jacopo Sannazaro* (1458–1530), the poet whose *Arcadia* depicts an ideal country of happy shepherds and shepherdesses; *Niccolò Machiavelli* (1469–1527), statesman, historian, and political philosopher whose *The Prince* was designed as a complete guide for rulers, instructing them how to retain their powers and authority by fair means or foul means, justifying deceit, brutality, and murder if necessary to serve the monarch or dictator; *Ludovico Ariosto* (1474–1533), whose romantic poem *Orlando Insane* includes genealogical and historical information about the Este family, which the author extolled in repetitious but melodious verse; *Baldassare Castiglione* (1478–1529), friend of Raphael and art collector whose *The Courtier* portrays the ideal courtier as soldier, artist, musician, writer, diplomat, refined lover of a gentle, cultured lady—the perfect gentleman; *Benvenuto Cellini* (1500–1571), famous craftsman in gold and silver, musician, and sculptor whose candid *Autobiography* relates his own life of dissipation and wild adventures and portrays the fascinating characters of many of his Italian contemporaries; and *Torquato Tasso* (1544–1595), poet and dramatist employed by Duke Alfonso of Ferrara, whose epic about the First Crusade, *Jerusalem Liberated,* depicts victorious battles, the capture of Jerusalem, and fantastic love stories involving brave knights and self-sacrificing ladies.

Writers in French were *Rabelais* (ca. 1494–1553), monk, priest, physician, educator, and author of the humorous satiric works *Gargantua* and *Pantagruel,* advocating a well-rounded humanist education; the philosopher and educator (previously mentioned for his skeptical philosophy) *Michel de Montaigne* (1533–1592), originator of the personal essay as a form of literature, author of numerous essays about human relationships, depicting the good and bad aspects of human character, customs, motives, ideas, and opinions, without condemning or praising himself or others; *Pierre Corneille* (1606–1684), attorney, poet, and dramatist who in his tragedies portrayed the passions and will of tragic heroes to whom the common people looked for spectacular exploits (as in his *The Cid,* a tragicomedy about lovers, family feuds, and victory for the brave); *Molière* (Jean Baptiste Poquelin, 1622–1673), traveling actor (befriended by King Louis XIV of France), the greatest of French playwrights, writer of lifelike comedies, including musical comedies, showing the true, selfish, and deceitful character of people such as physicians, aristocrats, and religious imposters and hypocrites; and *Jean Baptiste Racine* (1639–1699), poet, tragic dramatist, associate of the writer of fables, La Fontaine, and of Molière, aided by King Louis XIV of France, author of classical plays based on Greek traditions, stories, and characters, especially *Phèdre* patterned after the story of Euripides' *Hippolytus,* and other plays similarly depicting the consequences of sin, the need for moderation, and the reward of virtue.

Writers in Spanish were *Cervantes* (Miguel de Cervantes Saavedra, 1547–1616), a crippled Spanish soldier, captured and enslaved several years, sold as a slave, then ransomed, later imprisoned in Seville, where he began to write his masterpiece, *Don Quixote,* in jail, a novel depicting the differences between the dream world of chivalrous knights and idealized ladies (in medieval literature) and the real world of roguery, greed, illusion, and hypocrisy prevalent among all social classes; the anonymous author (1554) of the novel *Lazarillo of Tormes,* about the family history and adventurous life of a common but clever rogue and criminal, including descriptions of immoral clergymen, stingy priests, and unbelievable religious rituals and miracles, a work condemned by the Church and put on the Catholic Index of forbidden books; *Mateo Alemán* (ca. 1547–1610) of Seville, impoverished author of many works, especially the famous novel *Guzmán de Alfarache,* about a rascal, beggar, and crude adventurer who traveled widely in Europe and finally wrote his confessions when condemned to the galleys, exposing and condemning the immorality, manners, and customs of his acquaintances; *Lope de Vega* (1562–1635), priest, doctor of theology, survivor of the Spanish Armada, romantic adventurer, prolific author of epics, lyric poems, and more than 1,800 plays, including comedies, history plays, and romantic dramas, emphasizing the story element and portraying the behavior of kings, peasant girls, and lovers, with intrigues and cunning plots that became prominent features of Spanish drama, exemplified also in the plays of *Tirso de Molina* (ca. 1571–1648) and the moralistic plays of the Mexican hunchback *Alarcón* (ca. 1580–1639); and, finally, the soldier, priest, and dramatist Calderón (Pedro Calderón de la Barco, 1600–1681), whose masterly play (*Life Is a Dream*) develops the theme that human life is a mere preparation for a real life of eternity.

Writers in English were *Edmund Spenser* (1552–1599), the gifted poet who established the Spenserian stanza of nine lines and devoted two decades to writing his masterpiece *The Faerie Queene,* consisting of six books (and part of a seventh) praising the character and exploits of the noble hero, Prince Arthur; *Sir Philip Sidney* (1554–1586), statesman, classical scholar, writer of lyric poetry, including the pastoral romance *Arcadia,* the sonnets *Astrophel and Stella,* and critical comments on poetry in *An Apologie for Poetrie,* as well as translations—an English gentleman, lover of poetry, who took Greek classics as his models; *Francis Bacon* (1561–1626), statesman, essayist, philosopher, baron, Lord Chancellor, author of legal, literary, and philosophical essays universally admired, especially his *Novum Organum* on the philosophy and methods of science and his *The Advancement of Learning* on the various types of knowledge; *Christopher Marlowe* (1564–1593), atheist, opponent of conventional morality, father of English tragedy, author of numerous plays in blank verse, including *Tamburlaine the Great,* about the conquests and death of the Mongol warrior Tamburlaine, and *Doctor Faustus,* portraying a scholar who sold his soul to the devil; and *William Shakespeare* (1564–1616), actor, foremost dramatist and poet of all times, author of exquisite sonnets and thirty-seven plays, including histories, comedies, and tragedies (such as *Hamlet, Macbeth, Romeo and Juliet, Julius Caesar,* and *King Lear*) unequaled in their eloquence and power, depicting human beings of all types and classes, their character, motives, life situations, and fate, so that the ideas and language in the plays became ingrained in the hearts and minds of readers in all lands as potent educational influences and resources.

Other important writers in English in the seventeenth century were *John Donne* (1572–1631), a Catholic who converted to the Anglican Church, later Dean of Saint Paul's Cathedral, author of deeply philosophical poems about life, death, love, and immortality, and numerous witty and satirical poems; *Ben Jonson* (1573–1637), bricklayer's apprentice, soldier, actor, translator, writer of satiric plays, comedies, court masques, poems, and songs (for example, "Drink to Me Only with Thine Eyes"), whose most admired works are the comedies *Volpone, or the Fox* and *The Alchemist; John Milton* (1608–1674), poet, educator, author of political and religious treatises, including *Areopagitica,* his masterly defense of a free press, epic poems *Paradise Lost* (about good and evil, the fall of man) and *Paradise Regained* (about Christ and the story of man's redemption), and the drama *Samson Agonistes* (about the biblical Samson and his death struggle); and *John Dryden* (1631–1700), great poet, playwright, critic, satirist, master of English prose, and translator, convert to Catholicism, author of the fine comedy *Marriage à la Mode* and the tragedy *All for Love* (about Anthony and Cleopatra).

The following philosophers and writers devoted special attention to problems of learning and contributed significantly to the progress of education: François Rabelais, Michel de Montaigne, Francis Bacon, and John Milton.

FRANÇOIS RABELAIS

Rabelais was born in Chinon, a town in the province of Touraine, of middle-class parentage, one of five sons. He is said to have had a good elementary school education. He became a Franciscan monk, probably during his teens, residing at the monastery of Fontenay le Comte, where he studied Greek and classical literature. In or about 1519 he corresponded with the noted humanist scholar Budaeus, who persuaded King Francis I not to prohibit printing in France. Budaeus's letters indicated there was mutual distrust between Rabelais and the authorities at the convent. They resented his enthusiastic interest in Greek classics and other humanist studies, such as history and literature, even though Rabelais was also a diligent student of Scholastic philosophy.

Career of Rabelais. In 1524 Rabelais joined the relatively liberal Benedictine order and resided in one of their retreats for several years, but he eventually gave up this affiliation to become a secular priest. He matriculated at the University of Montpellier in 1532 to study medicine, earning the bachelor's degree within a few months' time; subsequently he lectured on the works of Galen and Hippocrates, some of whose writings he edited and translated into French. At about the same time he wrote one of his five popular books about the education, family backgrounds, and fantastic adventures of two gigantic kings (Gargantua and his son Pantagruel) and their vagabond associate Panurge. (In 1533 Calvin noted that the Church hierarchy had condemned the book as obscene.)

Rabelais worked as a physician at the local hospital in Lyons for about a year, then, in 1533, accepted a position as personal physician to Jean du Bellay, who was later appointed a cardinal and for some time protected him from persecution by the Church for anticlerical, humanist writings. Rabelais obtained his medical degree in 1537, became well known as a skilled physician, practiced dissection, and lectured on anatomy. For four years, beginning in 1539, he served as physician to Cardinal du Bellay's elder brother Guillaume du Bellay, the liberal governor of Piedmont, historian, statesman, and translator, who repeatedly defended humanists from clerical attacks. Guillaume du Bellay died in 1543, and Rabelais wrote a treatise in tribute to his late distinguished patient. He worked as town physician in Metz during 1546 and 1547, continuing to write his popular novels, protected by influential members of the du Bellay family against the criticisms of University of Paris theologians, who charged that his works were impious and obscene. Shortly before Rabelais died in 1553, the Sorbonne faculty condemned his fourth volume. (The fifth volume was published posthumously.)

Educational Ideas of Rabelais. The ideas of Rabelais on education are expressed in the first two books of his five volumes concerning the adventures of Gargantua, Pantagruel, and Panurge. His sources, from which he quoted freely, were ancient classical writings, including those of Plato, Vergil, Plutarch, Cicero, Pliny the Elder, Hippocrates, Galen, and the early Christian fathers, also contemporary works of Erasmus and other humanists, and all sorts of folk stories, ballads, even fairy tales, rough jokes, aphorisms, and puns. He developed his plots around the royal giants and Panurge, and described the education received or recommended by them. In these volumes Rabelais repeatedly condemned the rigid, gloomy, otherwordly curricula of the monasteries and extolled humanist views on behalf of classical scholarship and science, the free search for truths about man and nature, the creative arts (especially music, architecture, and poetry), history, language, philosophy, sports, games, and physical exercises, the full development of the individual in body and mind by means of firsthand experience in the natural environment, in the home, and in community affairs—all based upon the assumption that the acquisition of diversified knowledge will lead to the good life.

The royal giants described in Rabelais's five novels presented the elements of an ideal education, stressing the advantages of an all-round curriculum reflecting living realities and directed toward the enjoyment of life and learning, a curriculum designed to facilitate the mastery of truths and skills of every conceivable kind—cooking and other everyday tasks, facts about sex and biology, law, medicine, the whole panorama of studies from arithmetic to zoology, including Greek, Latin, Hebrew, Arabic, natural sciences, mathematics, music, world geography, ornithology, navigation, botany, world religions, the Bible in Greek and Hebrew, and skills needed for national defense. Nothing was to be excluded from the curriculum that might enrich the intellect, amuse, entertain, or satisfy the natural curiosity and practical needs of the learner.

Rabelais pointed up this philosophy of education with humor and crude jokes about clerics and Scholastic hairsplitters, hypocritical judges, wine drinkers who drink while debating about their thirst, cowards acclaimed for their acts of splendid courage, and every variety of burlesque and paradox; all the familiar aspects of thinking and experience among the common people were involved in the ideal education prescribed for the royal giants.

The humorous, earthy, satirical writings of Rabelais were extremely popular during his lifetime and long thereafter. Although they did not reform the static monastic programs or the narrow type of humanist practices in schools, they had a profound influence upon the ideas of later writers and educators, including Montaigne, Shakespeare, Locke, and Rousseau, thereby contributing to revolutionary changes in modern education.

MICHEL DE MONTAIGNE

Like Rabelais, but more tolerant of human frailties, Michel de Montaigne was a leading French writer, versed in Greek and

Roman classics, an independent-minded educator representing the characteristic spirit and ideals of the Italian Renaissance in opposition to the rigid otherworldly views of the Scholastics, a philosophical critic whose eloquent literary works had a profound influence on modern thinkers, authors, and educators in all countries of the Western world.

Life of Montaigne.   Montaigne was born in 1533 in the castle owned by his family east of Bordeaux in southwestern France. His mother was descended from a Spanish Jewish family. His father was a prosperous fish merchant, soldier, and prominent official in Bordeaux who saw to it that Michel studied Latin and Greek with a tutor and servants at home, all of whom, since they knew no French, talked with the boy in Latin. At six years of age, he was enrolled in a Bordeaux college staffed by famous teachers of the highest reputation. In his teens he studied law and became a member of the Bordeaux parliament, a post he relinquished in 1571 because of ill health. Thereafter he devoted himself mainly to the writing of his unprecedented *Essays,* a new form of literature treating every variety of human interest, consisting of three books, two of them published and immediately acclaimed in 1580, followed by revised editions in 1582 and 1587.

Montaigne served on the staff of King Henry III of France in 1574 and also in the retinue of King Henry IV. He traveled occasionally and wrote a journal of his travels to Italy, Germany, and Switzerland, partly in Italian, the remainder in French. In 1581, while improving his health at the baths in Lucca, Italy, he was elected mayor of Bordeaux, serving four years in that capacity. He devoted much of his time then and thereafter, however, to revisions of his previous works and to his third book of essays, published in 1588, four years prior to his death in 1592. The essays, based on his own life experience, classical readings—especially the works of Plutarch—and frank self-analysis, express conservative views in a skeptical yet kindly, tolerant style, discussing familiar ethical, emotional, and philosophical ideas and problems of mankind. His writings have been a source of inspiration to numerous modern philosophers and educators, including Francis Bacon, Shakespeare, Rousseau, Emerson, and Thoreau.

Educational Ideas of Montaigne. Montaigne did not entirely reject the comprehensive scholarly curriculum advocated by Rabelais, the languages and literature, arts, science, mathematics, and other knowledge derived from books. He maintained, however, that character development and the ability to evaluate one's own personality, to determine and fulfill one's own physical and spiritual needs, and to understand and cooperate with others are far more important educational objectives than the mastery of verbal or factual lessons. Learning should be natural, easy, and free. The student should be encouraged to practice virtuous conduct, to value true friendship and harmonious living with associates, and to avoid dogmatic conclusions or extreme opinions too often assumed to be infallible truths. In other words, the method of teaching should be directly contrary to that of the Scholastics and the humanists, all of whom depended mainly upon words and books instead of living realities.

Learning should be pleasant, not rigidly prescribed, not disciplinary or hard, and it should always be subjected to the test of life experience. The student should learn to live well as a gentleman, cooperating with like-minded people in the world of practical affairs. The best way to achieve this purpose, said Montaigne, is to employ a well-qualified private tutor instead of depending on class instruction in schools or colleges having prescribed, routine lessons from which the learner obtains little pleasure or benefit. With a wise tutor to guide him, the student will readily and enjoyably learn what he needs to know about the world of man and nature. He will learn to speak his native tongue well, become skilled in horsemanship, fencing, dancing, music, and whatever knowledge about history, government, law, medicine, and other studies will develop in him the marks of good breeding and the capacity to make appropriate decisions in personal and social affairs; in other words, he will learn how to live a good life wisely and well.

Montaigne believed in learning through practice—that is, putting information, impulses, and ideas into use repeatedly in practical situations instead of merely memorizing words or facts to repeat like a parrot to one's tutor. Such a philosophy of education was not suited to the formal curriculum of narrow humanist schools, and certainly not to the dogmatic programs of indoctrination emphasized in the monasteries. Montaigne's ideas naturally had little influence upon the schools he condemned, but his views were quite acceptable and popular among tutors employed in the homes of aristocratic French families. His main ideas were reinforced and supplemented a century later by the great English philosopher John Locke and another century thereafter by the revolutionary French philosopher Jean Jacques Rousseau, both of whom had a direct, pervasive impact upon education throughout the Western world during the eighteenth and nineteenth centuries.

FRANCIS BACON

Francis Bacon's writings popularized the inductive method of scientific investigation, turning the attention of educators away from medieval concepts about man and the universe, stimulating them to emphasize things in nature, instead of words, and to collect facts by means of observation and experimentation as a basis for scientific and educational principles and studies. He shared Montaigne's opposition to Scholastic authoritarianism but based his own views on systematized induction.

Life of Francis Bacon. Bacon was born into an aristocratic English family in London in 1561. His father, Sir Nicholas Bacon, a leading statesman during the reign of Queen Elizabeth, was devoted to education, a benefactor who supported a free grammar school and other educational causes. Francis was a precocious child, only twelve years old when he was admitted to Trinity College of Cambridge University. While at the college he concluded that the sciences being taught there were based on erroneous and inadequate methods, particularly the deductive logic and a priori conclusions of Aristotle, which had been accepted as the secret and core of knowledge throughout medieval and early modern times. (Church leaders and educators, and even Bacon himself, generally ignored Aristotle's inductive method—his practice of dissection and his advocacy of experiments and observation of facts.) Bacon, who studied and wrote fluently in Latin, was also a master of English prose essays, well equipped to communicate his views with force and dignity.

In 1575 he studied law at Gray's Inn and shortly thereafter became involved in political affairs. He served as a member of the House of Commons and, in 1591, associated himself with the Earl of Essex, who befriended him. When Essex plotted to depose Queen Elizabeth, however, Bacon condemned and prosecuted him, with the result that Essex was executed for treason. Notwithstanding Bacon's explanation that he had warned Essex not to oppose the queen, that he would be loyal to her, not to Essex, Bacon was attacked for betrayal of his friend. His condemnation of Essex helped to make him briefly a trusted adviser to Queen Elizabeth. When the queen died in 1603, Bacon ingratiated himself with her successor, King James I, to whom he dedicated his influential work on education, *The Advancement of Learning,* in 1605. For a time Bacon prospered, becoming solicitor general in 1607, attorney general in 1613, privy councillor in 1617, and lord chancellor and Baron Verulam in 1618. In 1621, however, the tide of fortune turned, when he was impeached by the House of Lords for bribery in connection with his judicial functions. He confessed and was fined and imprisoned, his political career in ruins even though the king remitted the fine, released him from prison, and granted a pardon. Five years afterward Bacon died of bronchitis.

The English poet Alexander Pope (1688–1744) called Bacon the wisest and meanest man of the times, but the times were evil and the majority of politicians were equally mean and grasping. Bribery was a common practice, rarely punished. At least Bacon wrote convincingly in behalf of the moral ideals he had betrayed. He denied that his judicial decisions had been changed by his acceptance of bribes and cited the fact that many of the donors had been convicted, yet he never refused or returned their gifts.

Bacon's Philosophy of Education.   Bacon was at his best as a critic of scientific and educational errors. The leading authorities on science, he asserted, were fundamentally mistaken because they ignored facts and experiments, the only valid method of investigating natural phenomena. He urged that the study of nature itself, not the a priori theories or deductive logic of Aristotle and the Scholastic teachers, be made the foundation of all sciences. He wrote his treatise, *Novum Organum* (*New Method*), to expound his view in opposition to Aristotle's deductive method of acquiring knowledge. He insisted that the authority of any authority, even that of the Church, must be rejected in all intellectual, secular matters and must be replaced by free, inductive investigation of nature. Facts must be ascertained, collected, compared, and used as the sole basis for the conclusions and principles of science. Moreover, they must be tested carefully, since a single negative result will disprove any conclusion despite a multitude of facts in its favor. The same method should be applied to learning in all fields. There must be no acceptance of alchemy, superstitions, unproved theories or explanations, fables, or magic, no hair-splitting debates about absolute truths, no mere dependence on books or authorities of any kind. The learner must depend on his own observation and experiments to discover real facts, effective causes and results, and observed events, not fanciful theories about what might explain natural phenomena. Educators, Bacon said, should teach the values of the inductive method of reasoning; in the sciences they should teach only the facts discovered and tested through careful experiments and observations. The road to knowledge begins with facts, which the senses ascertain from experience. Whatever is studied should pass the test of being true to nature's observed processes and man's deliberate experiments; whatever is true to nature so observed and tested will have practical value and will enhance human power over nature itself, thus advancing the cause of human welfare.

The student, said Bacon, should beware of the pitfalls of the mind, which often distorts and misinterprets the real causes and events in nature. He should reject prejudiced ideas or preconceptions and unproved traditional concepts, taking nothing for granted that has not been tested in the realm of sense experience, experimentation, and observation. He should be particularly careful not to be misled by ambiguous, misdirected, or dubious words, dogmas, a priori assumptions, and mistaken though plausible explanations of phenomena. He should not memorize the words or books of scholars as if they were gospel truths but should look to nature itself for provable facts. He should avoid futile disputes about mystical or useless issues, questions that have no practical significance for human society. Bacon wrote a utopian fictional work, *The New Atlantis* (1626), portraying an ideal society in which groups of scientists and scholars applied the inductive methods as a means of achieving true knowledge, happiness, and fulfillment. He did not object to or oppose revealed religion but declared that religious institutions should not attempt to solve problems of science. Revealed religion, he urged, should go beyond science and should be respected as a matter of faith not subject to evidence or proof.

The scientific and educational ideas of Bacon were deficient in that he failed to appreciate the vital role of hypotheses, tentative theories not readily amenable to an experiment, as possible explanations of observed data, and for this reason too hastily condemned the epochal discoveries and ideas of great scientists such as Copernicus, Galileo, and Harvey, who formulated reasonable theories about observed natural phenomena and eventually tested their theories by further observations or, where possible, experiments. The fact that his own influential writings were based upon reasonable hypotheses, not experiments on his part, proves that books and theories in books can disclose truths long before they are subjected to the decisive test of experimental application and experience. In fact, Bacon paid tribute to books (stating in his *Essays* that "some are to be tasted, others . . . swallowed . . . some chewed and digested"), noting that "reading makes a full man," pointing to possible truths not yet explored through induction and conclusions based on thoughts and feelings of great thinkers and creators of literature.

Unlike his contemporary, the famous philosopher Descartes, who was the leading mathematician of his time, Bacon failed to realize the value of mathematics as a tool of scientific investigation. He also failed to appreciate the inductive, experimental aspect of Aristotle's philosophy. He was not a competent experimental scientist and made no new discoveries. But he performed a significant service to science and education as a critic of authoritarianism, condemning the shortcomings of contemporary schools, the neglect of inductive methods of research and instruction, and the excessive dependence upon verbal, dogmatic, memoriter learning materials. His espousal of experimentation, free inquiry, and practical studies and the moral standards he defended in his splendid *Essays* had immense influence upon the thinking of later scientists, philosophers, writers, and educators. He was a most eloquent advocate of education as a means of transmitting learning and truth from one generation to the next. In his *Advancement of Learning,* he argued that men must not be skeptics or atheists and that they have a sacred duty to study the truths of the entire universe as the work of God, but with due humility, never assuming that they can rival God's mastery of the absolute or ultimate secrets of the universe.

JOHN MILTON

John Milton, the foremost pamphleteer of his time and one of the supremely gifted poets of all times, was born in London (1608), fortunate in having a father of the highest character, a scrivener by profession and an accomplished musician, who provided him with excellent tutors and sent him to the famous Saint Paul's School. At seventeen years of age, John Milton matriculated at Christ's College of Cambridge University, where he studied Greek and Roman languages and classics and the Seven Liberal Arts of grammar, rhetoric, logic, geometry, arithmetic, astronomy, and music and wrote superb poems that were widely admired. He earned the bachelor's degree in 1629 and the master's in 1632. Thereafter for six years he devoted himself to further study of the same subjects, continuing to write his masterly poems. He traveled in France and Italy during 1638, then returned to England and became a tutor of his two nephews and a few other pupils, soon involving himself in the religious and political controversies besetting the ill-fated regime of the tyrannical King Charles I. Charles was then engaged in a critical struggle with the Long Parliament for dominance, a contest ending with the civil war of 1642–1645 and the king's execution in 1649, an act that Milton vigorously defended.

Career of John Milton. In 1644 Milton wrote a treatise on education, setting forth his views concerning studies to be learned and methods of learning. In 1643 and 1644 he wrote pamphlets favoring the relaxation of divorce laws, which subjected him to violent attacks, especially by Presbyterian clerics, on the ground that his stand was immoral and his writings illegal, since they had not been licensed by censors.

Milton had hoped that the Long Parliament, which he had praised for having abolished the Court of the Star Chamber, notorious for its systematic imprisonment and torture of authors of unlicensed writings, would allow a free press. Instead the Long Parliament passed a new censorship law to be enforced by its own appointed censors. Milton defied the censors; issued his un-licensed pamphlets in 1643 and 1644 on divorce, violating the ordinance; and then addressed to Parliament his unlicensed speech *Aeropagitica* (1644), a bold defense of freedom of the press, stating that no opinion should be subject to censorship, that books are living things, that whoever "destroys a good book, kills reason itself . . . the image of God . . . the precious lifeblood of a master spirit, embalmed and treasured up on purpose to a life beyond life." He condemned the Roman Catholic Church for instituting censorship of books and he also broke from the Presby-terian clergy because they had favored their own style of censor-ship.

Milton's battle for press freedom inspired similar eloquent defenses of a free press in many lands, including America. In 1722 Benjamin Franklin, at sixteen years of age, commenting on his brother's imprisonment for a news release, declared that "without freedom of thought, there can be no such thing as wisdom, and no such thing as public liberty without freedom of speech." In 1734, when a British governor jailed Peter Zenger, editor of the New York *Weekly Journal*, because of his newspaper editorials, Zenger (ably represented by the noted attorney Andrew Hamilton) won the case by virtue of a liberty-loving American jury, a victory not forgotten during the controversies leading to the American Revolution. In England prior censorship did not end until the regime of William and Mary in 1689 when the arguments of British liberals, such as the great philosopher John Locke, won Parliament over to Milton's point of view concerning freedom of the press. In Western countries the complex problems of a free press and free speech remained controversial in the eighteenth, nineteeth, and twentieth centuries. In the United

States, during the 1970s, Milton's view against prior censorship of the press was successfully defended by the *New York Times* in the *Pentagon Papers* case.

In 1649 Milton's pamphlet defending the execution of King Charles I was followed by his appointment as an influential official propagandist (Secretary for Foreign Tongues) in the regime of Oliver Cromwell, whom he greatly admired; he held this position until 1659.

Milton had suffered from failing vision since 1644 and he had become totally blind in 1652; yet, with the aid of assistants, he continued to serve Cromwell well until the latter's death in 1658. The restoration of the monarchy under Charles II endangered Milton's life but, after being briefly imprisoned, he escaped execution and devoted himself to writing his literary masterpieces *Paradise Lost, Paradise Regained,* and *Samson Agonistes,* as well as the last of his pamphlets condemning the papacy, published in 1673, the year before his death.

Educational Views of John Milton. As Bacon had done, Milton advocated the teaching of useful studies in the student's native language although he, like Bacon, was a classical scholar who wrote fluently in Latin. Milton's proposed curriculum was not, however, based on Bacon's scientific method. Like the curriculum outlined by Rabelais, it emphasized practical subjects to be learned from classical sources—that is, from ancient Hebrew, Greek, and Latin writings. According to Milton, the student from the age of twelve to twenty-one years should learn the essentials of the following subjects from his reading of books: classical and modern languages and literature, including poetry; mathematics; natural science; economics; history; philosophy; physiology; geometry; politics; rhetoric; law; religion; agriculture; engineering; architecture; and physical education and health—and all other types of information that will have practical value in life.

Milton's *Tractate on Education,* which in 1644 recommended the organization of academies as secondary schools to provide such a curriculum, had a great influence upon the academy movement both in England and in the United States. In both countries the old Latin grammar schools had ignored or minimized practical subjects. In America, mainly because of Milton's point of view, many secondary schools introduced a considerably broader course of study than had been previously offered. During the eighteenth century numerous academies providing such instruction in the vernacular were organized, which were to become the forerunners of and models for modern American high schools. Benjamin Franklin adapted the ideas of Milton and the similar views of the leading British philosopher John Locke to the practical needs of American youth. He cited Milton and Locke as authorities in his plan for an English school as part of a pioneering academy in Philadelphia established in 1751.

Milton's program of instruction worked well for him and the few students he tutored, but it was considered far too elaborate and comprehensive for secondary schools of either the practical humanist or the Latin grammar variety. However, many new academies in England attempted to provide a broad curriculum including mathematics, modern as well as ancient languages and literature, history, economics, agriculture, astronomy, oratory, navigation, geography, logic, ethics, surveying, and other studies Milton had recommended. They also tended increasingly to teach in an informal manner so that the student would master the applications of useful information, not merely words or rules to be memorized and repeated to the teacher. Education, said Milton, should be designed to prepare youth for successful achievement in their private lives, their careers, and their civic duties.

WOLFGANG RATKE

In German lands during the seventeenth century great educators espoused the scientific views of Francis Bacon, emphasizing experience and experiments rather than books and literature (preferred by John Milton) as instruments of education. One of Bacon's contemporaries, the educator Wolfgang Ratke (1571–1635), a principal of schools in Moravia and Poland who had studied Baconian pedagogical ideas in England, attempted to apply them to classroom instruction in experimental schools at Augsburg, Köthen, Magdeburg, and other towns in Germany. Ratke, an impractical administrator, quarreled with the clergy and was briefly imprisoned by the government as an impostor. But he formulated and attempted to practice pedagogical principles based on Bacon's philosophy of induction that were far in advance of his time.

His principles of education advocated following nature as a guide in arranging the sequence of lessons; the study of all subjects through speaking, reading, and writing in the native language; systematic, frequent repetition of material being learned; mastery of one unit or lesson before going on to the next; insistence on order and attention to the teacher in the classroom; a question-answer method of ensuring comprehension of subject matter; direct contact with and investigation of objects and events in nature instead of merely accepting verbal authoritative opinions or answers in books or discussion; and encouragement of each pupil to progress at his natural pace so that he will learn to discipline himself, work independently, and put into practice what he has learned. Ratke advocated the teaching of all school subjects to the children of Germany in the German language, a policy designed to unite the states into a single nation. His ideas, elaborated in the widely acclaimed work *Methodus Nova* (*New Method,* 1617), had considerable influence on another renowned disciple of Bacon, John Amos Comenius.

JOHN AMOS COMENIUS

Comenius was a Moravian bishop and educator, born in a poor family in 1592, his parents being members of the Moravian Brethren, a persecuted Protestant sect prominent in Bohemia, Poland, and Moravia. The Brethren organized numerous schools emphasizing faith in God, rejecting the Catholic Church and hierarchy, and teaching moral conduct as evidence of true faith.

Career of Comenius. Comenius studied at the universities of Herborn and Heidelberg, then served as pastor and rector of schools of the order. During a period of religious persecution he fled to Poland, where he became the bishop of the Brethren, taught Latin, and wrote influential works on education as well as theological tracts. Other members of the Moravian Brethren found refuge in England, Saxony, and America. As their bishop,

Comenius helped to unite the various churches abroad, obtaining financial assistance for them and arranging for his own family members to become officials of the communion.

Comenius's methods of language instruction were unique, and his Latin texts were far superior to existing textbooks in that subject. The government of Sweden employed him as an adviser in its program of school reorganization. At Lissa, Poland, while engaged in formulating new educational plans for Sweden, Comenius was again compelled to become a refugee from persecution, and he settled in Amsterdam during the final years of his career. He died there in 1670.

Educational Ideas of Comenius. Many of Comenius's educational methods were remarkably modern, centuries in advance of prevailing practices. They had little impact on teaching methods or curricula of seventeenth-century secondary schools and universities with the single exception of his techniques of language instruction, which became popular in European countries. His text, *Janua linguarum reserata* (*Gates of Languages Unlocked*, 1631) was one of several popular works he published in this field, and it was widely used in German *Gymnasien* (secondary schools) for the study and teaching of Latin. A simple introductory section, the *Vestibule*, of a few hundred words, initially printed separately, constituted a first reader in Latin. His method of teaching any foreign language featured a working vocabulary of several thousand words in meaningful sentences, presenting useful facts in one column, and in a parallel column stating the same facts in the student's native language. Words and sentences were thus made significant to the learner, enabling him to comprehend information immediately and precisely. His textbooks presented graded lessons geared to the progress and needs of individual students. Conversation in the foreign language was a primary method of instruction.

Comenius also pioneered in illustrating his textbooks with drawings portraying specific facts, followed by statements of conclusions and general principles in accordance with the inductive logic advocated by Francis Bacon. The same method was utilized in Comenius's book for young children, the *Orbis Pictus Sensualium* (*The World of Sensed Objects in Pictures*, 1654), in which the child learned about nature and everyday objects of experience from pictures accompanied by and cross-referenced with numbers to the statements of information shown in each picture. Illustrations of water, the earth, buildings, circles, triangles, and the like clarified the text, giving the child meaningful concepts and systematically expanding his familiarity with and understanding of, not merely words, but also things and people in his natural and social environment.

Comenius's extraordinary summary of his educational ideas in *The Great Didactic,* written in his late thirties (published in Latin in 1657) stated basic principles of education that would be quite appropriate in the twentieth century, such as the following: (1) all children should receive adequate practical instruction, not from tutors or individually at home, but in common schools attended by pupils in groups organized according to their ages; (2) school lessons should follow nature and should be graded on the basis of each child's interests and ability to learn them; (3) the best foundations of learning are built in the early years of childhood; (4) the scientific method of induction from specific facts to broad conclusions or concepts should control the process of study and methods of teaching; (5) the essential aims of education include self-knowledge, self-discipline, and character development; (6) children expand their horizons, deepen their understanding of the environment, and learn best if they have firsthand experience with objects and social situations, learning every point thoroughly and accurately through practical use in life; (7) subject matter to be learned should be organized from ideas familiar to the child to the unfamiliar or new ones, from the simple ideas to the more complex ones; and (8) education should be given both to girls and to boys so that all children will realize their potential development into good citizens and virtuous God-fearing human beings. Comenius divided formal educational programs into four levels: (1) the *Mother School* for ages from infancy to six years; (2) the *Vernacular School* for ages six to twelve years; (3) the *Latin School* for ages twelve to eighteen years; and (4) the *University* for ages eighteen to twenty-four years.

During the latter part of the seventeenth century, in addition to Comenius, three prominent educators made significant contributions to educational theory and practice, namely, the Lutheran cleric *Augustus Hermann Francke* (1663–1727), the leading British political philosopher *John Locke* (1632–1704), and the noted French writer and prelate *François Salignac de la Mothe Fénelon* (1651–1715).

AUGUSTUS HERMANN FRANCKE

Francke, a Protestant theologian, was born in Lübeck, northern Germany, in 1663. He attended a Gymnasium in Thuringia; later studied Hebrew, Latin, and Greek at several universities; and graduated from the University of Leipzig, where he joined the faculty as an unpaid lecturer on the Bible, depending on students' fees for his stipend. Inspired by the renowned preacher P. J. Spener, he associated himself with the Pietist sect, a mystical, purely spiritual Christian religious movement, as one of its founders. His theological views, based on each individual's emotional acceptance of and exclusive faith in the Bible, aroused the vehement opposition of orthodox Church leaders and resulted in his expulsion as a lecturer at the University of Leipzig. In 1691, for the same reason, he was removed from the staff of lecturers at the universities of Erfurt and Dresden. Finally, in 1692, he joined the faculty of the new University of Halle as a professor of ancient languages and theology, serving also as a pastor in a nearby town and earning a wide reputation for his eloquent lectures and sermons, which continued until his death in 1727.

Like Comenius, Francke believed in formal education as an instrument for the realization of religious ideals. His theological and educational ideas were in many respects similar to those of Comenius, and he, too, attempted to put realistic pedagogical principles into practice. For this purpose in 1695 he organized the first of four types of schools, which he later called 'Institutions"—a school enrolling the children of the poorest classes (soon adding an orphanage). In this free school (the *Volksschule,* or school of the people) for very young children he formulated a curriculum including nature study, music, religion, the three Rs, history, and geography, taught in the native language. He then organized his second type of school, a tuition-paying school that developed into the Latin School (or Gymnasium), with a curriculum of mathematics, science, history, geography, music, Hebrew, Latin, and Greek. His third type of school was designed to serve the sons of the nobility as an advanced scientific school, the *Pädagogium,* equipped with science materials and laboratory facilities. The fourth type of school was a pioneering college for the preparation and training of prospective teachers, established in 1697 at Halle. (Father Demia had organized similar classes at Lyons, France, in 1672). Christopher Semler, a member of Francke's faculty at Halle, formulated a program of studies for secondary schools in 1739 with instruction in practical subjects, placing emphasis on agriculture, mathematics, drawing, and other studies useful in employment. This type of school program, which became the curriculum of the famous German *Realschule* (non-classical secondary school), was developed further in Berlin by Julius Hecker (1707–1768), a student of Francke, with classes in mechanics, modern languages, architecture, drawing, anatomy, natural sciences, accounting, mining, and manufacturing processes. The Prussian state owed much of its commercial and industrial progress during the eighteenth century to the spread of this new type of secondary school.

JOHN LOCKE

The renowned philosopher and educator John Locke initiated new trends in philosophy and education by means of philosophical essays in the seventeenth century, just as Francis Bacon had done in the sixteenth century. Locke's educational views, like Bacon's, were based on an Empiricist philosophy, which asserted that ideas are not inborn but arise from sense experience—that is, from sensations such as cold, hot, hard, soft, and yellow.

Life and Works of John Locke. Locke was born in the town of Wrington, England, in 1632. His father was an attorney who worked as a clerk for justices of the peace in Somersetshire and served as a captain in the army of the Long Parliament during the reign of the unfortunate King Charles I. Locke's father, a strict Puritan disciplinarian, believed that children should be supervised closely during their early childhood and thereafter should be allowed more liberty only when they demonstrate a capacity for self-discipline, a doctrine that Locke himself later defended as a valid principle of education. His father believed in political freedom and the parliamentary system of representative government, another view that Locke expounded in his influential writings.

In 1646 Locke, then fourteen years of age, was admitted to the exclusive Westminster School, where for six years he concentrated on the study of Latin and Greek languages and literature, among other customary secondary school subjects, and achieved a high academic standing. In 1652, matriculating at Christ Church College of Oxford University, he studied rhetoric, grammar, logic, moral philosophy, geometry, physics, history, Latin, Greek, Arabic, and Hebrew, earning his bachelor's degree in 1656 and his master's degree in 1658. In 1660 he was granted a fellowship as a senior student, with the privilege of remaining permanently at the university. Under the terms of his fellowship he worked as a university tutor in rhetoric, Greek, and philosophy. In 1665, during the restored monarchy under King Charles II, he joined a diplomatic mission to Brandenburg as secretary, returned to England in 1666, and then took up the study of medicine, soon acquiring a fine reputation as a physician. He successfully treated his distinguished patient Anthony Ashley Cooper, later prominent as the Earl of Shaftesbury and Lord Chancellor of England, who employed him as an adviser and arranged for him to live at the Cooper residence in London from 1667 to 1675. Until Charles II dismissed Shaftesbury as Chancellor for alleged favoritism toward Protestants, Locke served in the government as a secretary while retaining his status and privileges at Oxford University. In 1668 he was elected to the Royal Society of England, and it was then that he began to write his epochal work, *An Essay Concerning Human Understanding*. Shaftesbury became his lifelong friend, and upon his request Locke wrote a constitution (in 1669) for the British colony of Carolina in America. Both men advocated religious toleration and parliamentary government.

Locke suffered from chronic asthmatic attacks, which he cited as the reason for his travels in France during the period 1675 to

1679. In France he assisted the Whig political party (of which Shaftesbury was the head) to carry on secret discussions with the French in opposition to policies of King Charles II. Shaftesbury was imprisoned for plotting against the regime in 1676 and again in 1682, then took refuge in Holland, where he died in 1683. Locke was also suspected of participating in Whig conspiracies against the king although he had been careful to avoid public expression of his opinions. In view of the repressive atmosphere, however, he went to Holland, where he resided from 1683 to 1689. During this period of voluntary exile he wrote many letters counseling his friend Edward Clarke regarding the education of Clarke's son Edward Jr. These letters were later incorporated into his classic work, *Some Thoughts Concerning Education.* Clarke was arrested in 1685 (the same year in which the Roman Catholic convert James II, brother of Charles II, succeeded to the throne) for corresponding with Locke, whom the government branded as a traitor.

Locke continued his travels in Holland, participating in political activities in cooperation with other British refugees. In 1689 he returned to London on the same ship that in November of 1688 had taken William of Orange and the princess Mary to London to govern England, replacing James II, who escaped to France. In 1689 Locke's *A Letter Concerning Toleration* was published, to be followed in 1690 by publication of *A Second Letter Concerning Toleration* and his important philosophical works: *Two Treatises on Government* and *An Essay Concerning Human Understanding.*

Locke, now openly proclaiming his political views, held King William of Orange in high esteem, calling him a savior of the nation and guardian of parliamentary liberty. He was offered high posts in the government but accepted only lesser positions in order to continue his scholarly pursuits. In 1689 he defended the principles of a free press (more successfully than John Milton had done in 1644), with the result that the government finally abolished the law of prior censorship.

Locke's two treatises on government rejected the ancient doctrine of the divine rights of kings and asserted the natural rights of every human being to life, liberty, and the property produced by the labor of his own hands. These rights, he declared, were the fundamental reason for the existence of all governments. He advocated majority rule; government with the consent of the governed; the supremacy of the legislature over the executive; the division of powers among the legislature, executive, and courts; equality of all citizens under the law; taxation only with representation; and limitations on the powers of government over individuals. The powers of government, said Locke, are granted to rulers solely to enable them to implement a contract between themselves and the people. He justified the bloodless Glorious Revolution, which had deposed James II, and he defended rebellion against any government that refused to respect the natural rights of mankind. His writings inspired revolutionary leaders in America and France preceding the revolutions of 1776 and 1789. The preamble of the American Declaration of Independence and various clauses in the Constitution of the United States reiterated doctrines expounded by John Locke in his two treatises on government.

Locke's *Essay Concerning Human Understanding* held that the mind obtains knowledge from sense experience and is itself a passive recipient (a *tabula rasa,* or blank tablet) that absorbs from the senses many simple ideas, which combine or associate to form complex ideas. Locke formulated his doctrine of association of ideas, a term he coined and popularized, two centuries before the twentieth-century Russian physiologist Ivan Pavlov (1849–1936) and modern experimental psychologists developed the comparable principle of conditioning (the theory of learning through conditioned reflex actions of the central nervous system). Locke refused to speculate about the ultimate reality of the universe, the absolute substance causing sense experience and ideas, a problem analyzed but never fully solved by later philosophers, such as Bishop George Berkeley (1685–1753), the idealist who attributed all ideas to a divine mind, and David Hume (1711–1776), the skeptic who denied that anything exists except the experience of impressions that the mind makes into ideas.

It was Locke's view that the mind is restricted to its own ideas and cannot know the fundamental nature of the real substances represented by its ideas. He asserted, however, that real objects outside the mind possess the primary qualities of solidity, figure, extension, and motion, qualities that the mind perceives in the form of ideas or copies. Secondary qualities, such as colors, tastes, and smells, are not properties of real things but mere psychological creations. A stone has to be solid, have some shape, and occupy space, but it does not have to be black or red in order to exist. His explanations were unsatisfactory, nevertheless, since primary and secondary qualities appear to be equally ideas created in the mind.

In his discussions of ethics, morality, and religion, he advocated a hedonistic view that whatever is good gives pleasure and whatever is bad gives pain, and he agreed with deists that obedience to divine laws results in pleasure and happiness. At the same time he accepted Aristotle's conclusion that God, who created the universe, does not interfere in human affairs.

Locke's philosophical doctrines, despite their incompleteness and apparent inconsistencies, became universally popular and formed the basis for his influential principles of education and psychology.

In addition to the major works published in 1690, his noteworthy writings included: *Of Study* (1677); *A Third Letter Concerning Toleration* (1692); a treatise on interest rates and the value of money (1692); *Some Thoughts Concerning Education* (his classic work in this field, 1693); two treatises on the reasonableness of Christianity (1695); *Some Thoughts Concerning Reading and Study for a Gentleman* (1703); *Paraphrases on the Epistles of St. Paul* (1705); *Of the Conduct of the Understanding* (1706); and *A Fourth Letter Concerning Toleration* (1706). In 1699, five years before his death, a fourth edition of his most influential work, *An Essay Concerning Human Understanding*, was published. Throughout his career he had remained a steadfast opponent of authoritarianism in religion, government, and education, a staunch defender of religious, political, intellectual, and cultural liberty.

Educational Views of John Locke.   In his writings on education, Locke had in mind the practical needs of the sons of gentlemen in the upper classes of England, not the children of the common people. About women and the poor, he declared only that all should study the Bible and the skills required in their daily tasks. Nevertheless, his views had a great impact on the education of all children irrespective of their economic or social status.

Locke rejected the view (held by the ancient philosopher Plato and the modern philosopher Descartes) that ideas are innate. All learning, he said, is based on sensations and reflection. Children remember and learn through associating ideas derived from sensations. They remember ideas that naturally go together or in sequence, ideas that are repeated with understanding, ideas that bring them success, pleasure, and satisfaction.

Locke made a sharp distinction, however, between education and the mere acquisition (through association) of verbal information to be memorized and recited. The purpose of education, he insisted, is to develop in children all the powers of body and mind needed to make them healthy, virtuous, and successful in life. Bacon and Comenius had emphasized the information and knowledge to be acquired through inductive reasoning and experience by the learner; Locke emphasized the study of subjects that train the child's powers, faculties, and habits. The goal of education, according to Locke, is the achievement of a sound mind in a sound body, the "clay-cottage" of the mind. Mind and body are closely interrelated and cannot be separated. The very young child needs close supervision and strict discipline over mind and body to make certain that he learns to endure hardships or disappointments and forms fixed habits of right thinking and good behavior. As he grows older and demonstrates the ability to control his natural impulses and desires, he should be granted more freedom to go his own way and make his own decisions. In the guidance of very young children, however, discipline must not be so severe as to arouse in them animosity or hatred directed against their tutor or to discourage their interest in learning any useful subject. Disapproval and punishment should be natural, self-evident consequences of misbehavior. The tutor must never forget his duty to respect the child's opinions and personality, to disapprove and correct undesirable habits but also to encourage and approve correct reasoning and right conduct. The relationship among tutor, parents, and pupil should be one of mutual trust, reflected in the expression of candid, considerate opinions and in friendship accompanied by kindly discipline. If such a relationship exists, the child will readily accept correction, gradually develop high moral character, and increasingly discipline himself, habitually and spontaneously displaying qualities of temperance, diligence, consideration for others, kindness, fortitude, courage, and prudence.

These personality traits, said Locke, are far more valuable than the acquisition of information. In fact, memorized information should be kept within the bounds of the child's understanding and practical needs. Moreover, the tutor should stimulate interest in, and enthusiasm for, study and learning, adapt lessons to the child's capacity and preferences, and provide encouragement to facilitate the pupil's success and pride in accomplishment. Learning will then become as enjoyable and fruitful as play and games.

Locke's inquiry into the mental equipment and intellectual needs and activities of the individual child laid the foundations for modern empirical psychology, experimental psychology, and child study. His conclusion, however, that the mind is merely or largely a passive instrument receiving sense impressions stamped upon it has been rejected by psychologists. Critics have also attacked his view that the individual has mental faculties or distinct mental powers that can be developed best through the study of mathematics and similar "knotty and hard" subjects requiring "reasoning closely and in train . . . the way of reasoning" which man "might be able to transfer" to "other parts of knowledge as they have occasion." His emphasis upon repetition, habit formation, and the validity of transfer of training dominated school instruction during the eighteenth and early nineteenth centuries. Teachers consequently tended to stress drill work in classroom procedures, often ignoring Locke's admonition that clear thinking and understanding of learning materials are as necessary as repetition. To this day, disputes continue as to whether or not some children or even races inherit superior mental equipment, whether or not mental powers can be developed best through selected studies and then applied (transferred) by the learner to other studies, whether or not the natural impulses of the young child should be strictly controlled, as recommended by Locke, or allowed free rein, as advocated by the revolutionary philosopher and educator Jean Jacques Rousseau, who accepted and popularized many of Locke's other views on education and society. The eminent twentieth-century psychologist Edward Lee Thorndike (1874–1949) formulated psychological laws—the laws of readiness, exercise, and effect—which include and supplement Locke's principles of interest, repetition, and success in learning.

Locke declared that parents and tutors should serve as models, exhibiting superior qualities of character, such as virtue, wisdom, good breeding, and diligence, worthy of admiration and emulation by children. The child who attempts to imitate these models should be encouraged, praised, corrected, or redirected when necessary but never overburdened by excessive criticism or trivial assignments. Do not, Locke advised, try to stuff children's heads "with a deal of trash" they will never think about again "as long as they live." Education should be practical, purposive, meaningful, and enjoyable. The child must be respected, "treated as a man," allowed to express his opinions and to learn from experience, acquiring knowledge, powers, and skills that will be useful to him. Let him have adequate recreation and rest, said Locke, always let him know the reasons for rules and studies, and encourage him to develop self-direction and self-discipline.

Learning from experience is, according to Locke, far better than memoriter learning from books, but reading and language instruction must also not be neglected. Students should not be required to study hair-splitting arguments of theologians, but they should read the Bible with understanding and appreciation of its moral lessons. Subjects that require too much technical perfection or time for mastery, such as instrumental music, should not be prescribed, but dancing stimulates grace and self-assurance and merits priority in the curriculum. Children should be shown the world as it is, including its vices and dangers, so that they will realize what to condemn and avoid, what to praise and emulate.

According to Locke, there are individual differences among children in their capacities to learn and to develop physical and mental powers, as well as in their interests in and preferences for particular studies and activities. These individual differences should be observed and respected. Always, however, high standards of reasoning, communication, and conduct should be required. Locke condemned the narrow curriculum, low standards, and artificial tasks in contemporary Latin grammar schools, which emphasized the rote learning of Latin, Greek, classical literature, and religion. He advocated the teaching of reading, speech, English composition, drawing, handwriting, history, geography, mathematics (arithmetic and geometry), psychology (the nature of human nature), law, realistic literature (that is, plays, stories, and poetry true to nature, to human nature, and to life), moral philosophy, government, politics, natural philosophy, anatomy, chemistry, gardening, carpentry, and any studies preparatory to a career. He recommended independent travel (without a guide) and apprenticeship in vocations abroad, asserting that these experiences develop self-control, deepen the understanding of people, encourage habits of thrift and order, and enable the student to master foreign languages through reading, conversation, and practical use. His views won wide acceptance in England, France, and America during the eighteenth century. They helped to broaden the curricula of the old Latin grammar schools in England and America and to pave the way for the social and natural sciences in nineteenth-century academies, high schools, and colleges.

EIGHTEENTH-CENTURY FRENCH REFORMERS

In France during the eighteenth century leading writers and statesmen agitated for drastic reforms of education and society. In 1687, three years before the publication of John Locke's *Essay Concerning Human Understanding,* François Salignac de la Mothe Fénelon—the French prelate, archbishop of Cambrai, prose writer, and tutor of the grandson of King Louis XIV— published his treatise *On the Education of Girls,* a subject Locke had neglected. Fénelon's utopian and satirical writings displeased the pope and the king, resulting in repression and exile in his diocese, and presaged the breakdown of the Bourbon regime. He advocated many of the same principles delineated by Locke:

education for physical and mental health and powers, habit formation through discipline, instruction in useful studies, moral education through emulation and suggestion, and learning from firsthand experience to cope with duties in home and community. He was a pioneering thinker on the education of women. His ideas were widely accepted by the French people and had considerable influence in shaping the views of leading intellectuals and reformers in eighteenth-century France.

The most famous of the French reformers were *Charles Louis de Secondat, Baron de Montesquieu* (1689–1755), whose *Spirit of the Laws* (1748) compared varieties of government, favored a constitutional monarchy, and advocated the separation of powers in government as a safeguard against despotism; *Anne Robert Jacques Turgot* (1727–1781), statesman and economist, who as Minister of Finance approved of Locke's principles of self-government, equality of taxation under law, intellectual freedom, and toleration of Protestants, and proposed a system of public education for the people of France; *François Marie Arouet de Voltaire* (1694–1778), philosopher, essayist, playwright, disciple of Newton and Locke (whose love of reason and liberty he shared), who mocked and condemned the Church hierarchy, denouncing all bigotry, intolerance, war, injustice, censorship, and the tyrannical government of his time, protests for which he was persecuted, imprisoned, and exiled; *Denis Diderot* (1713–1784), dramatist, editor of a unique encyclopedia in which French scholars summarized all of contemporary knowledge and demanded the same equality, rights, and privileges for the common people espoused by Locke and Voltaire, principles resulting in the French Revolution of 1789; *Louis René de Caradeuc de La Chalotais* (1701–1785), French parliamentary magistrate whose *Essay on National Education* proclaimed the principles of universal public education free from religious bigotry, an educational program designed to prepare citizens for a democratic society; *Barthelemy Rolland* (1734–1794), *Marquis de Condorcet* (1743–1794), *Comte de Mirabeau* (1749–1791), and *Charles Maurice de Talleyrand-Perigord* (1754–1838), four leaders who condemned the private denominational schools of vested interests and proposed a national system of education; and, finally, the impetuous

Jean Jacques Rousseau (1712–1778), philosopher, writer, composer, educator, and revolutionary, whose spirited sentimental works recapitulated and supplemented Locke's political and educational principles, demanded the destruction of established theological, political, and intellectual institutions, and defended the rights of all people to life, liberty, and the pursuit of happiness.

JEAN JACQUES ROUSSEAU

It was fortunate for the cause of freedom that Rousseau lived when he did. Despite his impulsive temperament and extremist opinions, or indeed because of them, Rousseau inspired many leaders and common people in Europe and America with a new faith in liberty, equality, integrity, and fraternity. He served the masses of humanity as an apostle of revolt against elite masters. He incited revolution, which won for the Western world the supremacy of the popular will, control by the common people over their own destiny.

Career and Works of Rousseau. Rousseau was born in Geneva, Swtizerland, in 1712, the second son of Genevan citizens, French emigrés from Paris. His mother died soon after he was born. His father, Isaac, a watchmaker by trade and also a dancing master, had a violent temper and in a rage beat the elder son so severely that he left home and never returned. Toward Jean Jacques, however, Isaac Rousseau was indulgent and affectionate and taught the boy to read, discussing with him classical writings of Plutarch and Ovid, novels of Molière, and various historical works, but he also set an example of irresponsibility and indiscretion, expressing impulsive, unfounded notions about morality and society and displaying a lack of self-discipline that was emulated by his son throughout his career.

Rousseau's aunt, who took care of him until he was eight years old, was a highly emotional, unstable person, alternating in a haphazard fashion between excessive repression and complete indulgence. She inspired him, however, with a love of music, a study that he pursued, if not systematically or thoroughly, yet seriously enough to qualify him for work in later years as a proficient music copyist and composer.

In 1722 Rousseau's impetuous father, convicted of violence against a fellow citizen, fled to Lyon in order to escape imprisonment. Soon thereafter, at ten years of age, the boy went to live with an uncle, who sent him to school in a village near Geneva, where he studied Latin and other customary academic subjects. In 1724 he was apprenticed briefly and unsuccessfully to an attorney (Rousseau had a low opinion of attorneys, whom he described as "fee grabbers"), then was apprenticed again, this time to an engraver, who mistreated him severely until he rebelled and ran away, thereafter wandering through the scenic Savoy country, attempting various petty employment assignments for none of which he was well qualified. Eventually a Catholic priest recommended him to a new convert, a twenty-eight-year-old widow named Madame de Warens, who remained for some years both a mother and a mistress to the youth.

During a brief sojourn in Turin, where he was taught and accepted as a member of the Catholic Church (an affiliation he later repudiated), he finally obtained work as an engraver but was discharged for making love to his employer's wife. Employed as a footman, he stole some material and then blamed a young girl for the theft when it was discovered, a shameful episode he regretted deeply in later years. In 1736 he made his home again with Madame de Warens at a new residence in Les Charmettes. She tried in vain to enroll him in a seminary for training as a priest, an occupation that he later described as "rubbish." Madame de Warens then sent him to study music at the residence of a choirmaster, an arrangement lasting six months, after which he again wandered about the countryside, working occasionally as a music teacher and secretary. He returned once more to live with Madame de Warens for a period of two years, during which their erudite physician initiated Rousseau into Cartesian philosophy and the sciences, as well as the works of Locke, Montaigne, Newton, and Fénelon. In 1740 he joined the family of M. de Mably in Lyon as a tutor of their children, an unpleasant experience that illuminated for him many of the challenging problems of education.

In 1741 Rousseau journeyed to Paris to present a novel mathematical system of music notation to the French Academy of

Sciences, but it was rejected. In Paris, however, influential new friends assisted him to obtain a position as secretary to the French ambassador in Venice. As usual he soon quarreled with his employer and was forced to return to Paris in 1745, thereafter working as a music copyist and also as a secretary to wealthy benefactors. At this juncture he became acquainted with eminent French writers, including Diderot, for whose great encyclopedia he wrote articles on music. While working on music ventures he met a simple, uneducated, unattractive girl, Thérèse le Vasseur, a high-strung maidservant with whom he set up housekeeping and established a permanent relationship of loyal affection. In his masterful autobiography (published posthumously) he stated that she had borne him five children, whom he had forthwith placed in a home for foundlings. There is no proof, however, that these children ever existed.

Rousseau's first notable work, *Discourse on the Sciences and the Arts* (published in 1750), won a prize offered by the Academy of Dijon and brought him immediate fame. In this essay be blamed all social institutions for having corrupted the morals of naturally good and virtuous human beings, asserting that the sciences and the arts of civilization have been the sole causes of immorality, greed, depravity, and all other evils afflicting mankind. In 1752 his successful operetta, *Le Devin du village* ("The Village Soothsayer"), was performed for King Louis XV, but Rousseau rejected an opportunity to be presented at court as the composer even though an appearance would have earned him a royal pension. He journeyed to Geneva on a visit to his now impoverished friend, Madame de Warens, in 1754, at which time he resumed his Protestant affiliation (previously abjured) and then returned to France. In 1755 another of his popular essays, *Discourse on the Origin and the Foundations of Inequality Among Men,* was published; in it he pleaded for a return to the simple life of happy, primitive peoples who had no desire to amass wealth or power. In 1756 he wrote his partially autobiographical novel, *Julie, or the New Héloise* (published in 1761), extolling the goodness, spontaneity, and sincerity of the heroine Héloise and her lover and condemning society for their mistakes, misfortunes, and misdeeds. He also made enemies among the intellectuals by writing a commentary on the theater (*Letter to d'Alembert Against the Shows*) critical of stage performances and Voltaire, whom he thereby deeply offended. Thérèse and he had been living as guests at the country residence of the wealthy Madame d'Épinay in Montmorency, but Rousseau fell in love with Madame d'Houdetot, the sister-in-law of Madame d'Épinay, and was soon involved in quarrels that made an early departure the better part of wisdom.

Rousseau's subsequent major works were *The Social Contract* (1762), which defended political democracy, the natural, inalienable rights of the individual, and the primacy of what he called the "infallible will" of the people; *Émile* (1762), a fascinating semiautobiographical account of the ideal education he advocated for all children; and *The Confessions* (1781–1788), an autobiographical masterpiece that, despite numerous inaccuracies, candidly revealed the author's innermost emotions, admitting serious errors and personality defects, recounting relationships with women, and recapitulating the main events of his career.

Rousseau's writings had become popular, but they offended the Church and the government as well as his intellectual friends. In 1762 the French parliament condemned *Émile*, whereupon, hearing that he was about to be arrested, Rousseau fled to Switzerland. When the Geneva governing council also condemned his book, he announced that he was giving up his Genevan citizenship and denounced them and their entire regime. During the period 1765 to 1767 he was the guest of the noted philosopher David Hume in England, quarreled with him, and then returned to France, shifting from one place to another and beginning to display symptoms of mental instability. In his last years he completed the writing of *The Confessions* and also wrote some dialogues and a sequel to *The Confessions*. Thérèse and he were residing at the home of a wealthy friend in Ermonville, near Paris, at the time of his death in 1778.

Rousseau was a deist who believed in tolerance of all faiths provided that they do not conflict with the ideals and high moral standards needed in a representative democracy. He favored a democratic republic governed by the best-qualified elected representatives, who would govern for the benefit of the entire community, quite different from the "cheats" and "burglars" who manage affairs in a monarchy and seek only their own advancement. His views on government and education became effective weapons in the drive for revolutionary changes in modern political and educational institutions.

Educational Views of Rousseau. Rousseau's unprecedented basic principle of education stated that the education of children should conform to nature and to each child's individual needs. His natural impulses must never be restrained. The child is born good, said Rousseau, and he can acquire evil habits only from adults who misdirect him through harmful discipline and bad example. Rousseau approved of most of John Locke's educational views, but rejected Locke's recommendation of strict control over the very young child's desires and activities. He also rejected Hobbes's contention that man is born evil, corrupt, competitive, aggressive, and greedy and must therefore be controlled by means of laws and governmental powers. On the contrary, Rousseau asserted, man is born not only with a useful instinct of self-preservation but also with sympathy and good feeling for his fellows, beneficent qualities that civilization perverts so that the individual acquires artificial, immoral, unsound preferences and habits. Parents then treat their children as if they were miniature adults in the false belief that they are thereby preparing them for life, forgetting that every child is living here and now and needs only self-expression, activity, and freedom to build his physical and mental powers. Education must not be planned as a preparation for life, but only as an opportunity to learn from immediate, interesting, enjoyable life activities.

Trust nature, Rousseau advised, for it is a divine source from which all goodness and right living are derived. The best thing a parent or tutor can do for a child is to allow him to pursue his natural interests and preferences. The absolute rule for the education of very young children is to do nothing, to let nature do the teaching. The mother who obeys nature will breast-feed her infant. The father who sets an example of moral conduct and then lets his son alone to learn from experience—that is, from the natural consequences of his actions—is following the law of nature. Tutors who help the child to follow interests that lead to contacts with nature and attempts to overcome obstacles and hardships are properly respecting his individuality and normal mode of self-expression.

To help the child achieve self-realization and fulfillment, one must understand his physical, social, and intellectual characteristics, powers, and needs. Rousseau emphasized the necessity for understanding children, and he rivaled John Locke as a pioneer in building the foundations of modern child psychology.

Rousseau divided the life span of the individual into five periods or stages of growth and development, a type of analysis imitated by later educators and by twentieth-century psychologists, who postulated similar, though more detailed or precise, conclusions. A century earlier than Rousseau, Comenius had divided his educational program into four levels (up to six years, six to twelve years, twelve to eighteen years, and eighteen to twenty-four years), but Rousseau described his own divisions as natural stages of growth rooted in the physical, psychological, and social nature of the child. (Jean Piaget, the eminent twentieth-century Swiss educator, coeditor of the J. J. Rousseau Institute of Geneva, and defender of Comenius's views, postulated three stages of human growth.)

Rousseau's *first stage of growth* is that of infancy and very early childhood—that is, from birth to five years of age—during which the father can tutor the child while the mother nurses and cares for him—provided, however, that neither interferes with his natural impulses and habits except to stimulate his body movements, reactions to the environment, and mode of self-expression. The child will quickly learn what he needs to know as he gains strength, breathes fresh air, and withstands obstacles or pain, just as nature intends him to do. A child who behaves in a deceitful or unnatural way should simply be ignored, although if he cries, some means of distracting his attention is permissible. But, Rousseau warned parents, do not force him to behave as an artificial, perverted adult; let nature teach him. Keep him away from doctors, who know nothing about nature's own hardening and healing processes, and be sure to avoid their dangerous medicines. With all young children, said Rousseau, avoid artificial playthings and silly language, keep their toys and play natural and your conversation with them simple, direct, and honest.

In the *second stage of growth,* from five to twelve years of age, the emphasis should be placed on training the child's senses and body through experiences such as measuring distances, observing the changing phenomena of nature, using geometry and drawing to develop powers of observation, studying vocal music, which will increase his appreciation of harmonious sounds, exercising the muscles in sports such as swimming and jumping, and further hardening the body by exposure to the elements. Do not hurry the child, Rousseau urged, or try to shortcut the learning process by giving him books to read, which are not needed for his activities. If he breaks something, do not repair it but let him use it despite inconvenience to himself so that he will suffer the consequences of his mischief. A person whose property he destroys should retaliate in kind. Never preach to a child about morality, for he will not understand your reasoning. He can learn morality only through example and experience.

During the *third stage of growth,* from twelve to fifteen years of age, said Rousseau, let the boy investigate and discover for himself the laws of nature and science, how and why the seasons change, the working of electricity, the measurement of temperature with thermometers, the way to build and use tools and other practical things, just as Robinson Crusoe did in Daniel Defoe's classic tale, the only book the boy should read during this period of his career. He should learn a trade—such as carpentry, cabinet-making, or grain threshing—requiring the skillful use of hands and brain, for then he will be able to earn his own livelihood anywhere and will be happy, knowing that he cannot be enslaved by any employer. He will now have developed good, practical judgment about the way in which life situations can best be met for his own benefit, for the avoidance of pain or disappointment, and therefore for his true happiness. He will discover all these things for himself and will not have to depend on the authority of parents, teachers, or others in order to make the proper decisions. From practical experience he will develop accurate judgment, and since he will have formed no prejudiced theories or false preconceptions about the world and its people, he will make fewer mistakes than the scientists who keep changing their so-called "truths" from one generation to the next.

During Rousseau's *fourth stage of growth,* from fifteen to twenty years of age, the youth undergoes important social, moral, religious, and physical experiences, involving especially the maturation of the sex function and new relationships to other individuals. He must adjust his emotions and actions ("self-love") to the interests of his fellows. Personal contacts will usually awaken his sympathy, a "true" or "fitting" love and friendship for others, but he can also learn much from the study of history and even from stories that illuminate human motives and behavior. Observing the deceitful tactics of cheats and schemers, he will begin to appreciate the evil consequences of such conduct. Observing the good deeds and religious life of liberal persons serving the oppressed classes of society, he will understand the need to protect weak, poor, and defenseless victims of social conditions. He will accept and cope bravely with hardships and disappointments without complaint. Thus he will develop a truly religious spirit and form good moral attitudes and habits. For all such learning the example set by parents and tutors is essential. Formal religious or ethical doctrines will be of little use to him unless they reinforce the truths revealed by his contacts with people and by life situations. Through conversation and practical use, not through rules or grammar, he will learn to communicate effectively in his native tongue with others, a skill of the greatest value for establishing rapport with them.

In the *fifth period of his development,* now having become a man in his twenties, the individual needs to find a suitable permanent companion, a woman who possesses the character traits and skills required for the performance of her duties. Rousseau held that women should be taught mainly to be loyal, treasured wives and mothers. He recommended physical education to enhance their health and beauty; education in the arts, especially music and dancing, to make them attractive to men; training in domestic tasks, such as sewing and embroidery; and moral education, through religious studies and constant discipline from early childhood, so that they will become obedient, faithful, patient, gentle, and submissive companions. Individuals are mortal and die, he said, but the state endures; therefore, women must be strong enough to bear healthy children and perpetuate the race. This aspect of Rousseau's educational philosophy has been widely condemned on the ground that he misunderstood the many-sided nature of women, their genuine physical, psychological, spiritual, and social qualities and needs. His advocacy of special training for the functions of wifehood and motherhood, however, has often been accepted in practice as one phase of a broader educational program for women.

Rousseau was characteristically inconsistent in his views on public education. He demanded representative government subject to the general will of the people; yet he asserted repeatedly that the masses are poor and ignorant and do not need the kinds of educational opportunities he recommended for the upper classes. He was also misled into overdependence upon inborn impulses as the sole guide to the ideal education of very young children, underemphasizing the capacity of parents and teachers to control the physical and social environment so that it will reinforce or modify the child's innate tendencies.

Rousseau's attacks on artificial social institutions, excessive discipline, arbitrary authority, and impractical studies were aimed at the destruction of traditional obstacles to an ideal education. His more positive influences included the impetus he gave to the beginnings of child psychology, a new emphasis upon nature study and activities, self-expression, emulation, self-discipline, physical education, and the adaptation of teaching procedures to the individual differences, interests, and needs of children. He inspired many educators, writers, and philosophers, including, among the earliest of them, Johann Bernhard Basedow (1723–1790), Immanuel Kant (1724–1804), Jean Paul Richter (1763–1825), and Friedrich Froebel (1782–1852) in Germany and Johann Heinrich Pestalozzi (1746–1827) in Switzerland. The emphasis of John Milton, John Locke, and Jean Jacques Rousseau on useful studies and intellectual freedom stimulated the movement for practical subjects in the curriculum under the leadership of eighteenth-century statesmen and educators, especially Benjamin

Franklin (1706–1790) and Thomas Jefferson (1743–1826), in America.

JOHANN BERNHARD BASEDOW

Johann Bernhard Basedow, son of a hairdresser in Hamburg, Germany, graduated from a Gymnasium in that city and then matriculated at the University of Leipzig to study for the ministry, but instead he concentrated on philosophy. Later he was employed as a tutor in a family of the nobility in Holstein. He became well known for his teaching skill and was appointed as a teacher of moral philosophy in a Danish academy. His dissenting views on religion soon led to his discharge from that post and also from a similar appointment in a secondary school, whereupon he devoted himself to writing books concerning educational reforms based in large part on Rousseau's works. In 1768 he published an appeal to European community leaders and governments to establish a new type of public nonsectarian school for teaching practical subjects to all children, including those in the poor and middle classes. The public schools in any country, he maintained, should be under the control of a central government board of education. Interested subscribers contributed funds to enable him to publish several textbooks in dialogue form on elementary school subjects and a volume of illustrations to accompany the lessons. Pedagogical suggestions for parents and teachers were contained in another book on methods of teaching, his *Methodenbuch,* which recapitulated and exemplified many of Rousseau's ideas. These writings became very popular. Parents everywhere were dissatisfied with the artificial, inefficient methods of contemporary schools which imposed severe discipline and attempted to fill children's minds with useless rules or abstract statements. Many community leaders, already influenced by the teachings of Locke and Rousseau, welcomed Basedow's fresh approach to education.

In 1774 Basedow established a school at Dessau, Germany, named the *Philanthropinum,* which became the model for numerous similar schools throughout German lands. He adopted some of the principal ideas of Comenius and many ideas of Rousseau: children should be understood as human beings on their own level, not as if they were adults; the course of study should include music, dancing, drawing, games, sports and physical exercises, geography, mathematics, physics, and history; young children should be allowed to move about freely and noisily, instead of being repressed; instruction should in most instances be given in the native language; the teacher should connect lessons with real things and experiences, not with abstract ideas or statements; discipline should be natural and moderate, excluding formal lessons in denominational religion or in morality; languages should be mastered through actual use in conversation and reading; and children should wear clean and comfortable clothing, not stiff uniforms.

Basedow's school was visited by outstanding community leaders from many countries, who praised his ideas. His textbooks delineated the new, practical materials and methods of instruction in detail, but he himself was an irresponsible, impetuous, inefficient administrator, failings that eventually ruined the *Philanthropinum*. Basedow resigned as director in 1778, then taught private pupils and continued writing on pedagogical topics until his death at Magdeburg in 1790. The *Philanthropinum* closed in 1793.

IMMANUEL KANT

Immanuel Kant (1724–1804), one of the most profound philosophers of modern times, praised Basedow's educational ideas and experimental school. Even after becoming somewhat disillusioned by the deficiencies of the school, Kant advocated similar experiments in education, and in his own work, *Regarding Education,* he praised the freedom allowed teachers and pupils by Basedow as the only means whereby improved methods of instruction could be developed. Kant accepted Rousseau's doctrines that the general will of the people must govern political decisions, including those of war and peace, and that individuals in all countries should be free to think, speak, and move about as they please. He declared that children could become morally responsible adults only if they were free to make up their own minds instead of being coerced or indoctrinated by grownups. Each person should learn to respect the intelligence, individuality, and welfare of all others. No human being should control the will or decisions of another individual. Kant acknowledged the conflict that often arises between the impulses and reasoning of the young child. He disagreed with Rousseau's conclusion that very young children cannot reason correctly about moral questions, stating that only through experience and attempts to use his intelligence can the child develop clearer understanding and greater self-discipline. The newborn, said Kant, is neither good nor bad, but he soon begins to form concepts of order, law, and duty, and he will do this best through free activities and practical experiences, such as those advocated by Rousseau and Basedow.

CAMPE, SALZMANN, ROCHOW, AND ZEDLITZ

Two of the teachers in Basedow's *Philanthropinum* were Joachim Heinrich Campe (1746–1818) and Christian Gotthilf Salzmann (1744–1811). Campe succeeded Basedow as director of the school for about a year, then founded a *Philanthropinum* in Hamburg. Campe translated some of the works of Locke and Rousseau into German and in 1779 published a popular book for children, *Robinson Crusoe Junior,* a prototype for a famous story-book published by Johann Rudolph Wyss (1781–1830), *The Swiss Family Robinson.* (Basedow and his staff had written a number of such storybooks for young children containing moral lessons, religious anecdotes, and nature-study materials.) Salzmann founded a *Philanthropinum* in 1784, which emphasized instruction in gardening, agriculture, the care of animals, geography, physical training, religious lessons, and reading; the school remained influential in German lands for over a century. Salzmann also wrote numerous pedagogical guides for teachers.

Baron Eberhard von Rochow (1734–1804) organized schools like Salzmann's, designed to teach children farming and basic academic subjects. As Basedow had done, Rochow agitated for a centralized system of nonsectarian public schools under government supervision and control.

Frederick the Great, the liberal ruler of Prussia, fostered education and science, decreed compulsory schooling for children five to fourteen years old, as well as continuation schools for older children, and established state authority over education in 1763 and 1765. In 1771 he appointed Baron von Zedlitz, who approved of Basedow's and Rochow's educational programs, to be the head of Lutheran Church and School Affairs. Zedlitz broadened the curriculum of German schools and founded a normal school for the training of teachers. In 1787 he organized a central board of education. The civil laws in 1794 transferred control of education from the Church to the state, providing for a centralized national nonsectarian school system, the system of universal education that had been advocated by Basedow and Rochow. School programs were placed under the supervision of government inspectors, and teachers could be employed only with the approval of state authorities. Other German states followed the example of Prussia.

FRANKLIN AND JEFFERSON

The ideas of Locke, Rousseau, and Basedow spread to the American colonies before the end of the eighteenth century and assisted leading statesmen, such as Benjamin Franklin (1706–1790) and Thomas Jefferson (1743–1826) in their efforts to achieve freedom of expression and universal public education. Eminent Americans—including John Jay, chief justice of the United States Supreme Court; Dr. Benjamin Rush; Thomas Paine, revolutionary philosopher and author; and Presidents George Washington, John Adams, and James Madison—joined the campaign for public education. Even before the close of the eighteenth century, a few state constitutions proclaimed the value of public education. Unfortunately, the disastrous economic effects of the Revolution and the vested interests of Church schools and private schools delayed major steps toward the establishment of nonsectarian, tax-supported common schools in many states until the second and third quarters of the nineteenth century.

Franklin led the way in Pennsylvania, Jefferson in Virginia. In

Pennsylvania William Penn's visionary program of 1683 for universal education did not materialize; parochial schools predominated, as the Quakers organized schools, some for boys, others for girls, and various other religious sects, attracted to the colony by the tolerance shown by Penn and his successors, also formed schools of their own. In Virginia numerous endowed local secondary schools were founded early in the eighteenth century (a few decades after the comment of its British governor William Berkeley that "learning has brought disobedience and heresy and sects into the world"). They were supplemented by individual instruction of apprentices in trades and limited manual training for children of the lower classes.

Contributions of Benjamin Franklin. Benjamin Franklin, statesman, author, journalist, inventor, philosopher, and educator, was born in Boston, Massachusetts, in 1706, the son of a devout Puritan candlemaker and his second wife, parents of good character and reputation who taught the boy to read and later enrolled him (at eight years of age) in the Boston Grammar School (the Boston Latin School) as a first step toward study at Harvard College for the ministry. Despite an excellent academic record, Benjamin remained at the school only one year, for his father had become dubious about the cost and value of a college education. Enrolled the next year at a business school, the boy failed in arithmetic, ending his formal education.

Beginning in 1718 Franklin worked four years as a printer's apprentice to an older half brother, James, who treated him harshly. Subsequently he settled in Philadelphia (1723) and struggled through many hard experiences as a journeyman and master printer. Through independent study, he developed extraordinary facility as a writer. At sixteen years of age he wrote anonymous essays critical of the educational program of Harvard College; they were published in his brother's weekly journal and attracted wide attention. His first major work was *Poor Richard's Almanac,* the most popular publication in the colonies, begun in 1733 (under the pseudonym Richard Saunders) and issued over a period of twenty-five years as an annual compilation of astrology, weather predictions, current events, verses, notices, proverbs, and commonsense advice about temperance, order, frugality, justice, moderation, cleanliness, and other virtues. His masterful *Autobiography* (begun in 1771, published in part in France in 1791 and in its entirety in 1868) inspired young people for over a century as evidence of what they could achieve by means of honest, diligent work and self-discipline in America, their land of opportunity.

Many volumes would be required to describe in detail Franklin's extraordinary career and influence during the decades 1720 to 1790.

In 1729 he purchased and for eighteen years published *The Pennsylvania Gazette,* a weekly journal in which he defended ideals of liberty, freedom of speech and press, peace, brotherhood, and intellectual and religious toleration (stating his own dedication as a deist to reason instead of authoritative theological dogmas).

In 1731 he formed the first subscription library in America, a library for public use, containing classical literature as well as practical works. In 1735 he planned and soon thereafter organized the first police force and in 1736 the first fire company in the colonies, the Union Fire Company of Philadelphia. Also in 1736 he served as clerk to the Pennsylvania Assembly. In 1737 he became the deputy postmaster of Philadelphia. In 1739 he invented the famous Franklin wood-burning stove, a great improvement in the heating of rooms, not surpassed even in the twentieth century.

In 1743 he became a founder of the American Philosophical Society, an outgrowth of a Philadelphia discussion club (the Junto), which he had formed in 1727 and which was imitated in many foreign countries. In 1749 he founded the Academy in Philadelphia, which opened in 1751 and eventually developed into the University of Pennsylvania.

In 1751 he published the results of his pioneering experiments in electricity, and in 1752 he invented the lightning rod planned in 1749. In 1753 he discovered the positive and negative forces in electricity, and he received the Copley medal for numerous electrical discoveries. In 1754 at the Albany Congress called by the British government, he proposed the Albany Plan for union with England, including representative government, taxation only with representation, and equitable treatment for Indians. In 1756 he was elected a fellow of the Royal Society.

In 1763 he published a pamphlet on the black people of Pennsylvania, stating that blacks equal whites in every respect, including intelligence and learning ability. In 1764 he published an appeal against the mistreatment of Indians, who, he said, must not be penalized merely because they have "a reddish brown skin and black hair." In 1764 he was elected Speaker of the Pennsylvania Assembly. In 1766 his testimony before the House of Commons influenced the British government to repeal the Stamp Act.

In 1774 he met with Thomas Paine in London and urged him to go to America, where Paine's writings helped to unite the American people before and during the war for independence. In 1775 he served as a delegate to the Second Continental Congress. In 1775 he became Postmaster General of the American colonies. In 1775 he joined Thomas Jefferson on a committee to write the American Declaration of Independence, drafted mainly by Jefferson, and became a signer of the Declaration. In 1775 he drafted Articles of Confederation in an attempt to unite America and Britain. From 1776 to 1785 he served as an American envoy to France and made successful arrangements with that country that were a decisive factor in the outcome of the Revolution of 1776. In 1776 he induced Thomas Paine to write the pamphlet *Common Sense,* which swept through the colonies as an effective weapon in the battle for liberty.

In 1780 he invented bifocal eyeglasses. In 1781, together with John Jay and John Adams, he negotiated peace terms that ended the war against Britain officially in 1783. From 1785 to 1787 he was president of the Pennsylvania Executive Council. In 1787 he became president of the Pennsylvania Society for Promoting the Abolition of Slavery. (During the last year of his life, 1790, he petitioned Congress to abolish slavery and wrote a sharp satire against the slave trade.) In 1787, despite failing health, he served as a delegate to the Constitutional Convention, during which he advocated the right of Congress to overrule a presidential veto and the right of Congress to impeach the president. He helped frame the "Connecticut Compromise" on the makeup of the

House of Representatives and the Senate, which saved the Constitution of the United States, and his final appeal to the delegates ensured its ratification.

Although Franklin accepted John Locke's philosophy of education, he applied its basic ideas not to the sons of English gentlemen, as Locke had done, but to the children of all classes of society. The colonies needed skills in agriculture, mechanical trades, business and commerce, and government; therefore Franklin propagandized for Locke's favored curriculum of useful studies, such as the three Rs, English language usage, mathematics, bookkeeping, geography, history, government, physical training, the natural sciences, farming, carpentry, and other vocational subjects, all to be taught mainly through experience and practice, supplemented by books. Study of the classics and the Bible, Franklin asserted, need not be neglected, especially the moral aspects to be absorbed from them, but the core of the curriculum for most children should consist of studies designed to serve their practical needs and the needs of their communities.

Franklin agreed with Locke that even the basic skills and practical knowledge to be derived from education are less important than the development of high moral character, habits of clear and logical reasoning, integrity, and self-discipline. He considered education, science, and government necessary instruments enabling individuals better to serve their fellows, their community, the nation, and mankind. Franklin's influence, exerted through his writings, school and library programs, community services, liberal views, and personal example, contributed materially to the advancement of universal public education, a broader program in the Latin grammar schools, and the organization of numerous academies, similar to his prototype English school of 1751. Thus the way was paved for the vast expansion of American secondary education in general high schools, technical schools, and vocational schools.

Contributions of Thomas Jefferson.   Thomas Jefferson, third president of the United States, lawyer, musician, scientific agriculturist, athlete and horseman, author, and educator, was born at Shadwell, in Albemarle County, Virginia, in 1743. His father, an engineer, justice of the peace, and prominent legislator, was a dedicated democrat who inspired his son to emulate his liberal political and social ideals.

Jefferson was educated at the College of William and Mary and early demonstrated meticulous scholarship in classical and modern languages and literature, mathematics, and the natural sciences. A skilled violinist and singer, he was also an expert sportsman, proficient in dancing and horsemanship. He studied law for five years after graduation from college and was admitted to the Virginia bar in 1767, thereafter displaying exceptional analytical ability that was responsible for major improvements in the legal system. In 1769 he was elected to the Virginia House of Burgesses. In 1772 he published a significant treatise, *A Summary View of the Rights of British America,* which set forth fundamental principles of self-government for all parts of the British empire and the natural rights of Americans, and declared that the king of England had exceeded his authority by vetoing legislation in the colonies, by preventing the abolition of slavery, and by quartering armed forces on American lands. Jefferson also declared that parliament had exercised powers beyond its rightful jurisdiction, especially by hampering the free trade of the colonists. Jefferson's treatise was widely acclaimed. In 1775 his draft of the Declaration of Independence was adopted, reiterating the principles of his treatise of 1772. He served as governor of Virginia from 1779 to 1781, a member of the Continental Congress from 1783 to 1785, American minister to France from 1785 to 1789, United States secretary of state from 1790 to 1793, Vice President of the United States from 1797 to 1801, and President of the United States from 1801 to 1809, at which time, having refused to accept nomination for a third term, he retired to his plantation in Virginia.

Jefferson admired Benjamin Franklin and agreed with him concerning the basic aims and methods of education, views he could readily appreciate, for he himself was a disciple of John Milton, John Locke, and Jean Jacques Rousseau. As a firm adherent of democratic, local self-government, he advocated universal, public education supported by local taxation, a system he believed to be essential for the creation of an informed electorate and the preservation of a democratic republic. In Virginia he drew up and successfully advocated a law guaranteeing religious freedom and the separation of Church and state. In 1779 he proposed legislation to establish a central system of public education for the state, which would include three years of free elementary schooling for all children, advanced education for gifted students, a free state library, and a state college. His proposal was not implemented, owing mainly to the reluctance of prosperous planters to assume tax burdens that would be necessary in order to educate children of the poor, but in 1819 he founded the University of Virginia, which became a model for many similar American state universities. Like Franklin he pleaded for the eradication of slavery and for the equalization of political, social, and educational opportunities throughout the nation, ideals only partially achieved during the nineteenth and twentieth centuries.

JOHANN HEINRICH PESTALOZZI

John Locke had emphasized the disciplinary type of education whereby the child would develop a sound body in a sound mind through sense perception, closely supervised study of useful subjects, and the formation of good moral habits. Jean Jacques Rousseau had emphasized the naturalistic type of education whereby the child would develop physical and mental powers through contacts with nature and free self-expression, and moral character through emulation and life experience. The visionary Swiss educator Johann Heinrich Pestalozzi combined these two emphases in his educational theory and practice. Attempting to implement Rousseau's naturalistic doctrines, he soon discovered that children require not only contacts with nature and free expression of innate impulses, but also sympathetic guidance in their contacts with nature, in their observation of things, and in their reasoning and conclusions concerning experience. He then formulated his own theories and specific methods of instruction. Most important, he declared his faith in the loving care and education of all children, including those of the poor and handicapped, as well as the sons of Locke's English gentlemen and Rousseau's French aristocrats, as the best means to eradicate the evils of society.

Career and Literary Works of Pestalozzi. Pestalozzi was born in 1746 in Zurich, Switzerland. His father, an Italian Protestant, a prominent surgeon, died when Johann was only five years old, and the boy was reared in poverty by the widow and a loyal maidservant. He attended elementary and secondary schools, including the *Collegium Carolinum,* a school of advanced studies founded in the eighth century that had been revived as a humanist school during the sixteenth century by the liberal Swiss religious reformer and classical scholar Ulrich (or Huldreich) Zwingli (1484–1531), previously mentioned as a Protestant dissenter during Luther's time. At the college, Pestalozzi studied Greek and Hebrew languages and literature, history, rhetoric, and philosophy with progressive-minded professors who encouraged his idealism and interest in social reforms. He read Rousseau's works and wrote essays on political and social problems for a periodical sponsored by members of the faculty, gaining a reputation among conservative governmental authorities as a radical. Shortly thereafter, perhaps recalling Rousseau's description of lawyers as fee grabbers and his praise of farming as an ideal, natural occupation, he abandoned plans for a legal career and decided to become a farmer. For a year he received practical training in agriculture at experimental farms in the canton of Berne in west-central Switzerland. In 1768 he raised enough funds to purchase his own land and began to experiment with improved agricultural methods.

Pestalozzi's farming venture ended in 1774 as a complete financial failure owing mainly to his impracticality in financial matters. Consequently he converted the farm, which he had named *Neuhof* (*New Farm*) into a home and elementary school for abandoned beggar children of poor farmers in the vicinity. The pupils, numbering at first twenty, later as many as fifty, boys and girls, combined their work of gardening, weaving, cooking, sewing, and the like with group discussions and the study of the three Rs and the Bible. Although the children made remarkable progress and prospered, being well fed and clothed by Pestalozzi, and steadily improved in knowledge, skills, health, and character, the school had to be closed in 1780 for lack of funds. In this philanthropic venture Pestalozzi lost his own investment and his wife's inheritance so that only the aid of a few remaining friends enabled him to retain ownership of the family home. His only source of income was an occasional fee for writing articles on education and society for a journal published by a loyal friend.

In 1774 Pestalozzi had written a detailed record of the methods he had used at home to educate his three-year-old son in accordance with the educational principles set forth in Rousseau's *Émile.* Now he decided to devote himself to writing as a career. His noteworthy early writings included a journal article, *The Evening Hours of a Hermit,* printed in 1780, which spelled out his principal pedagogical views in the form of aphorisms. In 1781 he published the first volume of the novel *Leonard and Gertrude,* a widely acclaimed best seller that brought him worldwide fame and citizenship in the French Republic, an honor he shared with George Washington and Thomas Paine. Three additional volumes of the novel, however, were too complex for a popular audience and attracted few readers. Several other books he wrote on educational and social problems were similarly disappointing. He tried publishing a paper featuring news, comments, stories, and poems to expand his ideas. Other writings included *Illustrations for My ABC Book* (1787) and a philosophical treatise on human nature and education (1797).

In 1798, disenchanted with his writing career, Pestalozzi accepted a position as a teacher in a convent of the Ursuline order at Stans, a village in the canton of Unterwalden in central Switzerland. His seventy pupils were orphan boys and girls from the rebellious neighboring canton of Nidwadden whose parents had been massacred by the French army. Despite severe handicaps, particularly the animosity of local Catholics toward him as a Protestant teacher and the sad condition of the children, many of them ill with disease and distrustful of strangers, Pestalozzi, devoting himself wholeheartedly to their care and to the implementation of his pedagogical principles, met with astonishing success. His program featured nature study, excursions, and recitations combined with spontaneous activities of the children, object study, and manual labor. They were all kept busy observing, reciting, conversing, working, and learning as a cooperative group. He encouraged brighter and older pupils to help the others to understand and to learn. In mid-1799, however, even though the Swiss government honored Pestalozzi for his accomplishments at the orphanage, the French closed the school and converted it into a military hospital.

Pestalozzi then obtained a position as a teacher in Burgdorf, a village in the canton of Berne, teaching the three Rs to a group of twenty-five very young children through simplified, graded activities, and winning high praise from the local school commission. He then served several months as master of a local school for older children who proved difficult to discipline and too sophisticated for his simple step-by-step graded lessons in history, geography, writing, arithmetic, and the Bible. The government then permitted him to use a castle in Burgdorf for pedagogical research, the training of teachers, and the development of instructional materials. Assisted by an experienced associate and a competent staff of young teachers, he organized a pioneering institute and school. The institute produced textbooks and teaching manuals reflecting Pestalozzi's educational theories and methods. At this time (1801) he published one of his most influential works, *How Gertrude Teaches Her Children,* a book of letters recounting his early teaching experiences and expounding his principles of education.

The school at Burgdorf was an extraordinary success, admired by visitors from many lands eager to witness Pestalozzian methods of teaching. Again, however, his work was disrupted when Napoleon eliminated the central government of Switzerland. In 1804 the new government of the canton, antagonistic to Pestalozzi, ended his experiment at Burgdorf.

For a short time he associated himself with Philipp Emanuel von Fellenberg, a like-minded philanthropist and educator. Later in 1804, with the cooperation of authorities at Yverdon in southwestern Switzerland who had provided a place of refuge for some of his Burgdorf associates, he organized a school in a castle owned by the town. Once again his methods achieved unprecedented results for several years despite financial difficulties and laxity in administration.

As in his previous experiments, however, success turned into ultimate failure. Some critics of the educational program accused Pestalozzi of applying old pedagogical ideas while claiming that they were his own innovations. Others charged him with inciting revolution. Rivalries and dissension within the faculty compounded his financial and political difficulties until in 1825 the school had to be closed. Pestalozzi retired to his old home in Neuhof, where in 1826, the year before his death, he wrote his last publication, *Swan Song,* summarizing and defending his philosophy of education.

Educational Views and Methods of Pestalozzi. In European schools during the eighteenth century, the vast majority of children of the common people either had no educational opportunities or were kept in bleak, unhealthful, oppressive schoolrooms under the supervision of untrained, unpopular, and unsympathetic teachers who flogged them whenever they displayed their presumably wicked nature by failing to memorize and repeat their set prayers verbatim or to answer routine questions about the Bible, the core of the curriculum. Mutual antipathy was the prevalent relationship between schoolmaster and pupils. There could scarcely be any greater contrast than that between conditions in a typical school of that era and the ideal educational situation described in Rousseau's *Émile.*

Education for Social Reform. Pestalozzi's goal was twofold: to rescue children from the unwholesome, restrictive, and often brutal treatment to which they were subjected; and to pioneer in developing their natural powers and character traits so that they would become capable, conscientious citizens equipped to eradicate the evils of society. His main objective was therefore to achieve social reform through a new approach to education, a psychological approach based upon the innate abilities and natural potentialities of every child. Through the right kind of education, individuals would, he believed, develop the necessary health and strength, mental powers, knowledge, skill, and moral character to create the good society depicted in his influential writings, such as *Leonard and Gertrude* and *How Gertrude Teaches Her Children.* All children, irrespective of their social status, should be cared for, respected, and helped to develop their inborn natural physical and mental powers, faculties, and love for other people. The relationship between child and teacher must be like that between child and mother so that learning and teaching will become a shared process motivated by friendship, cooperation, mutual aid, and love.

Every child, said Pestalozzi, needs to express himself freely, to exercise his natural physical powers and mental faculties, and to learn from nature, from companions, from parents, from teachers, and from experience. In the home a mother's affection for her children induces them to heed her requests, to emulate her behavior, and in this way to grow and learn. Consequently the mother is the best of teachers. A good teacher follows the mother's example. Thus a good home and a good school create a good community.

PESTALOZZI'S PRINCIPLES OF EDUCATION.   Pestalozzi's methods of instruction were based upon his general conclusion that learning should begin with sense perception, observation, and contacts with nature—that is, experience instead of words or books. The learner must be guided by a sympathetic teacher, one who understands children as well as the subjects to be learned. Every pupil needs careful guidance in selecting what natural objects and phenomena to observe and what relationships to watch for in his contacts with nature. Pestalozzi spelled out this view by formulating definite principles of teaching, especially the following: education should be based upon child psychology; every child develops physically, mentally, and morally through experience consisting of sense impressions, careful observation, clear understanding, and the use of knowledge in his everyday activities; learning must progress through induction from the simplest to the more complex elements, from concrete things to abstract ideas, from what has already been learned to the next stage in an orderly arrangement or sequence and always from experience to judgments, conclusions, or rules; and teachers should consider and respect the individual child's interests, his readiness for further learning, his need of free self-expression and activity, and his other emotional and social needs so that he will develop naturally in physical strength, intellectual faculties, and moral character. Discipline and order are necessary, but they must be imposed only with justice and to help the children to learn, never merely to punish errors or penalize shortcomings. A teacher who is properly trained to use correct methods of instruction will keep children interested and active, making harsh discipline unnecessary.

Basic principles of instruction advocated by Pestalozzi are reflected in modern methods of teaching school subjects, such as arithmetic, language, geography, drawing, writing, nature study, physical education, handwork, and music. His classroom procedures were often inconsistent and impractical, but they included approaches and devices widely used in the late nineteenth and early twentieth centuries. His special methods in arithmetic, language, and geography typify his views. The youngest pupil studying arithmetic observes and handles pebbles, leaves, and other objects and thus discovers the meanings of numbers and begins to understand the relationships among them. He groups objects into pairs, in this way learning that four is the same as two plus two. He forms judgments about numbers, not as abstract symbols or words, but as qualities of real things. He uses pictorial designs, dots, lines, and squares, as well as objects; he consults computation tables in pictorial forms that make number meanings and relationships evident; he groups and separates real numbers to explore their relationships; and, finally, he states his knowledge, not memorizing or reciting combinations by rote, and, most important, applies what he knows to life situations, as in spending money and weighing and measuring objects. In studying language, the child learns at home the sounds of speech as expressions of emotions and indications of activities within the family. He will soon understand his mother's words, imitate her, and speak effectively about familiar objects and situations of interest to him. Conversation and practical use, said Pestalozzi, are the natural ways to learn any language. Geography study should begin as the child observes phenomena in his immediate neighborhood (for example, earth features, storms, streams, dew), then continue with observation and discussion (using models and map exercises) concerning phenomena in more distant places, political geography, statistics, astronomy, and play or games, illustrating the effects of geography on people and events.

Pestalozzi's Successors. Pestalozzi's disciples were extremely influential in many Western countries, especially in Germany, France, Britain, and the United States.

In Germany the racist philosopher Johann Gottlieb Fichte (1762–1814), a nationalistic forerunner of Hitler, advocated Pestalozzian ideas and pleaded for a national system of education based on them to unite and regenerate the nation as a "pure" race (a view directly contrary to Pestalozzi's ideal of human brotherhood) after the defeat of the Prussian army by Napoleon in 1806. His plea was fruitful in Prussia, which transferred control of education from the Church to the state, modeled common school programs along Pestalozzian lines, and established standards for the training and recruitment of teachers in the secondary schools. Carl August Zeller (1774–1847) organized a training school for prospective teachers and propagandized for Pestalozzian methods in the Prussian elementary schools. Similar activities by Friedrich Adolf Wilhelm Diesterweg (1790–1866) were particularly effective. Pestalozzi's friend and associate Philipp Emanuel von Fellenberg (1771–1844), head of a Pestalozzian school at Hofwyl, Switzerland, and interested primarily in agricultural and trade education for the children of the poor, combined academic education with manual training and vocational instruction. This program spread from Switzerland to Germany, Britain, and the United States, giving impetus to agricultural and industrial education for deprived and handicapped children. Pestalozzi's ideas had the greatest influence upon the most famous German educators—Johann Friedrich Herbart (1776–1841) and Friedrich Wilhelm August Froebel (1782–1852).

In France, notwithstanding ecclesiastical control, Pestalozzian ideas were spreading, and within a few decades the directors of education Victor Cousin (1792–1867), Baron Georges Cuvier (1679–1832), and Premier François Guizot (1787–1874) had adapted programs of elementary education to accord with many of those ideas.

In Britain the Welsh philanthropist and educator Robert Owen (1771–1858), the eminent Scottish jurist Henry Peter

Brougham (1778–1868), and the Reverend Charles Mayo (1792–1846), a prominent schoolmaster, adopted Pestalozzian views in their own theory and practice.

In the United States enthusiastic exponents included the Scottish-American geologist William Maclure (1763–1840); Joseph Neef (1770–1854), a former teacher on Pestalozzi's staff and organizer of a Pestalozzian school in Philadelphia in 1806, and a collaborator with William Maclure and Robert Owen at New Harmony, Indiana; and leading educators thereafter, including Horace Mann (1796–1859), Henry Barnard (1811–1900), Edward A. Sheldon (1823–1897), William Torrey Harris (1835–1909), Colonel Francis W. Parker (1837–1902), G. Stanley Hall (1844–1924), John Dewey (1859–1952), and William Heard Kilpatrick (1871–1965). Pestalozzian ideas were put into practice by Sheldon as superintendent of schools in Oswego, New York, where the new ideas became central features of the teacher-training program, emphasizing sense perception, object lessons in science, mental arithmetic, and instruction (though excessively formalized) in music, drawing, and handwriting; by Harris, who as superintendent of schools in Saint Louis, applied the object lessons of Pestalozzi to instruction in nature study and science, introduced the first public school kindergarten (1873), and served with wide influence as United States Commissioner of Education (1889–1906) and editor-in-chief of *Webster's New International Dictionary* (1909); by Parker, who as head of the Cook County Normal School in Chicago pioneered in the redirection of elementary education, developed Pestalozzian methods of instruction in geography as the core subject, and advocated Froebel's emphasis upon self-expression and spontaneous learning activities; and by Dewey in the experimental elementary school at the University of Chicago and later at Columbia University, where some of his followers developed the *progressive education movement* that was particularly influential during the 1930s and 1940s.

JOHANN FRIEDRICH HERBART

The noted German philosopher and educator Johann Friedrich Herbart (1776–1841), a student of Fichte at the University of

Jena in eastern Germany, was a brilliant classical scholar who taught philosophy at the University of Göttingen for several years. He then succeeded the renowned Immanuel Kant as professor of philosophy at the University of Königsberg, where for over two decades he gave courses in pedagogy as well as philosophy, and organized a practice school to implement his ideas on the psychology of learning and train prospective schoolteachers for service in Prussian schools. During the period from 1833 to the time of his death in 1841 he taught philosophy again at the University of Göttingen. His contributions to psychology, social ethics, and education had enormous influence upon educational theory and practice in the nineteenth and early twentieth centuries.

Herbart's Rejection of Faculty Psychology. Several years of experience as a tutor of children in Switzerland familiarized Herbart with practical aspects of teaching pupils who differ widely in ages, interests, and capacities. He visited Pestalozzi's Burgdorf institute and wrote a defense of Pestalozzian ideas, especially the aim of educating the poor and the idea that teachers should guide children toward systematic observations and experiences favorable to self-development, but he did not accept the faculty psychology of the great Swiss educator. He asserted that the development of moral character and ethical human relationships is the proper aim of education, and he held that innate propensities (or instincts) do not include an array of separate mental faculties but only the ability of the mind (as a single, unified entity) to compare, combine, and submerge ideas. His views on the aims of education were most fully elaborated in his notable work *The Science of Education* (1806). His textbook on psychology appeared in 1816 and his *Outlines of Educational Doctrine* in 1835, issued in a new edition in 1841 shortly before his death.

Herbart's Psychology of Learning. Herbart formulated the theory of apperception (the theory of apperceptive masses) to explain how ideas originate and interact in the mind. According to this theory, ideas that are similar reinforce each other and persist in consciousness, whereas ideas that are dissimilar compete with each other for attention so that one of them is excluded from consciousness (for example, when the idea of white excludes or contradicts the idea of black). This aspect of Herbart's theory resembles the conclusion of the twentieth-century psychoanalyst Sigmund Freud concerning the disappearance of ideas and experiences for specific reasons into the unconscious realms of the human mind.

Herbart explained that the individual thinks with his past ideas, the sum total of his previous experiences, and fits them into new ideas and learnings or habitual actions. The material learned in the classroom must therefore be presented in an orderly sequence. By relating new ideas to old ones already familiar to the child, a teacher can awaken his interest in the new ideas and enable him to associate them with ideas previously acquired, an aspect of associative memory emphasized by Plato in his *Phaedo* in the fourth century B.C.

Herbartian concepts of apperception and associative learning became widely accepted guiding principles in the preparation of classroom lessons. According to Herbart, learning materials prepared on the basis of apperception will clarify and enrich the learner's understanding, deepen his interest, and help him to retain new ideas in his memory. There is implicit in this view an approximation to the principle of readiness for learning (an experiential background) elaborated by the twentieth-century psychologist Edward Lee Thorndike on the basis of his scientific experiments in the field of animal learning. It is also similar to the principle of conditioning propounded by the great Russian physiologist and Noble laureate Pavlov, who concluded that the association of ideas is the primary element in memory and learning.

Herbart's Views on the Purpose and Methods of Education. In contrast to some of his followers, Herbart himself was not opposed to all "scattered" memorization of separate facts or to the need on occasion for hard work and self-discipline by the pupil, and he did not intend to advocate making all aspects of study a mere game of association of ideas at every point. He insisted, however, that the teacher can and should plan materials of instruction so carefully that the learner will become interested in step-by-step mastery of new ideas and will be well equipped to undertake new tasks. Moreover, the child should be so well guided by his teachers and their assignments that he will systematically form new ideas successfully in many fields of subject matter and will thereby become an educated person, possessing many interests and knowledge that will induce him to act in a worthy manner, confidently yet with humility, to form good habits, to develop civic virtues, and to achieve high ethical character. For this purpose, said Herbart, history, geography, languages, and literature (especially Greek literature, such as Homer's poems about heroic men) should be emphasized in the curriculum, albeit without neglecting mathematics and the natural sciences. All studies should be clustered around a core curriculum aimed at character development.

Herbart described the psychological means whereby the learner acquires new ideas and knowledge as a twofold process: (1) absorption of new facts or ideas; and (2) reflection about the new facts or ideas, or assimilation. Herbart's disciple *Tuiskon Ziller* (1817–1883) formulated five formal steps, modifying Herbart's own scheme of four steps, as the correct method of learning, called the method of the recitation: (1) preparation of the learner for the new material; (2) presentation of the new material; (3) comparison, association, and abstraction, noting similarities and differences of old and new ideas; (4) generalization, that is, the idea resulting from the integration of new with old ideas; and (5) application, or the use of a newly acquired idea in life situations and in further learning.

Followers of Herbart. Besides modifying Herbart's list of formal steps in learning, Tuiskon Ziller in Leipzig wrote an influential treatise (1865) that popularized Herbartian theories of education. (Ziller also formulated less successfully a culture-epochs theory, which states that the individual passes through stages of mental growth parallel to stages of human evolution, and he devised an elementary school curriculum built around literature, such as fairy tales, legends, and the Bible.) *Karl Volkmer Stoy* (1815–1885) followed Herbart's methods in a teacher-training school and practice school (1874) at the University of Jena. *Wilhelm Rein* (1847–1929) at the same university wrote or edited numerous volumes expounding Herbartian theories and familiarized many students from the United States and other countries with Herbart's methods. American normal schools accepted Herbart's theories and procedures. In 1892 the National Herbart Society was founded by leading American educators, including *Charles De Garmo* of Cornell University, *Charles A. McMurry* of Illinois State Normal University, and *Frank M. McMurry* of the Columbia University Teachers College. In 1902 the National Herbart Society became the National Society for the Study of Education, a change reflecting the declining popularity of rigid Herbartian procedures. Among influential works in favor of Herbartian theories were *The Essentials of Method,* by De Garmo; *General Method,* by Charles A. McMurry; and *The Method of the Recitation,* by Charles A. McMurry and Frank McMurry.

The formalistic, mechanical methods of learning advocated by Herbart's followers belied the naturalistic ideas of Rousseau, underemphasized spontaneaus activities of pupils, and made the teacher an authority or even an autocrat whose prearranged lesson plans became rigid patterns dictating procedures of instruction and learning experiences. Educators in a democratic society generally feel that children need experience in making free choices as well as obeying reasonable rules and orders if they are to become free, effective, self-governing adult citizens; that they should make some of their own creative plans and decisions, individually and cooperatively, with the advice or assistance of a democratically minded teacher. The same criticism has been leveled against the programed teaching and self-teaching devices of the twentieth-century psychologists S. L. Pressey and B. F. Skinner, whose predesigned step-by-step learning materials may reinforce effectively the pupil's mastery of certain subject matter but also require him to follow a plan that frequently becomes quite boring and may even impair his ability to create new ideas and solve his own problems in life situations.

Nevertheless, Herbart raised anew the question of how children learn, think, and grow, and his introspective analysis, while one-sided in its approach, stimulated modern psychologists and educators to investigate all aspects of the psychology of learning as scientifically as possible. He was an influential forerunner of experimental and educational psychologists and creative teachers who conduct and evaluate experimental programs of instruction in our contemporary schools.

FRIEDRICH FROEBEL

The renowned German educator Friedrich Wilhelm August Froebel (1782–1852), founder of the modern kindergarten, was, like Herbart, an influential follower of Pestalozzi, but he rejected Herbart's reliance on intellectual learning and the Herbartian teacher's role as an authoritative master, and instead emphasized play, self-activity, and learning by doing, the spontaneous interests and creative experiences of children.

Life of Froebel. Born in the village of Oberweissbach, Germany, in 1782, deprived of his mother in early childhood and neglected by his father, the pastor of the village, Froebel lived with an uncle in a nearby locality and attended the village school. He was regarded as a dull child, apparently because the routine, humdrum classroom lessons failed to interest such a boy, whose imagination turned his attention to observation of the wonders of nature and to mystical ideas about a divine spirit perfusing and unifying the universe. In his youth Froebel worked for two years (1797–1799) as an apprentice to a forester in Thuringia, an occupation that permitted him to search out the secrets of nature, observing the obedience of all plant and animal life to its laws and becoming determined to study and master their applications. With great difficulty he succeeded in attending classes at the University of Jena for about a year, but found the lectures unsatisfying. Furthermore, he was so poor that he suffered a brief imprisonment for debt. He worked several years thereafter in minor employments as a land surveyor, accountant, and the like, until he at last found his true vocation in teaching.

From 1805 to 1807 he served as a teacher in Frankfort on the Main at a Pestalozzian school, then for two years as a private tutor at the Yverdon Institute of Pestalozzi before returning to his studies, this time at the University of Göttingen and later at the University of Berlin. He served in the Prussian army in 1813 and returned the following year to work as a curator of a museum in

Berlin. Finally, in 1816, he opened a school of his own with only five pupils (a niece and nephews) in a tiny Thuringian village. Soon thereafter he moved the school to the village of Keilhau, which became the center of his unique educational experiments. In his major treatise, *The Education of Man* (1826), he described his principles and methods of education as they applied to very young children, mainly those from one to seven years of age, inclusive. From 1831 to 1836 he organized and directed successful elementary and secondary schools in Switzerland, including schools at Wartensee, Willisau, and Burgdorf, all aided by the Swiss government despite the opposition of the Catholic clergy. He concluded, however, that the education of younger children would be the most effective means of developing their natural powers and character. In 1837 in the village of Blankenburg he organized for such children the first school of its kind and in 1840 named it the *Kindergarten* (garden of children).

Froebel's *Mutter- und Kose-Lieder (Mother Play and Nursery Songs,* 1843), a collection of songs to accompany games, reflected the pedagogical methods delineated in his treatise. Despite the success and fame of the Blankenburg kindergarten, however, financial difficulties forced it to close within a few years. Froebel then devoted himself to lecturing throughout Germany on his educational theories. In 1849 he obtained assistance from the baroness Berthe von Marenholtz-Bülow, who permitted him to establish his educational center on her estate. The baroness became the foremost propagandist for Froebel's ideas in many European lands. Unfortunately, because of some confusion between Froebel's views and the socialist teachings of Karl Froebel, his nephew, the Prussian government concluded that he himself was a revolutionary and in 1851 forbade the organization of kindergartens in the nation, a humiliation inflicted one year prior to the death of this greatest and noblest benefactor of all the world's children.

Educational Views and Influence of Froebel. The educational theories of Froebel were based on his belief in the unity of nature, in the reality of universal natural laws, and in a divine spirit governing the life of man as a part of nature. The child, he said, should observe, study, and work with nature, including plant and animal life and nonliving objects, so that he will gain a clear understanding of the ever-changing forms of life on earth as well as the laws of inorganic nature. Froebel believed that an eternal law rules and pervades all things in the universe, unifying them in a divine system, and that the child, through his study of nature and his free self-activity in the kindergarten, will learn about the natural world, his fellow human beings, and his own character and identity as a divinely created being. The child's nature is such that he is able to think, act, and grow by expressing his inner desires, interests, and powers.

Froebel agreed with Pestalozzi that children are born in possession of specific mental faculties, but he asserted that growth, power, and self-fulfillment develop from the child's inner impulses, through spontaneous activities. Thinking, he said, is one kind of activity, and thinking is involved with other forms of doing, as in play, gestures, speech, song, and motor expression. Knowing and doing are therefore aspects of the same inner activity of self-expression and creative living. As plants grow from within, aided by nature, so the child will unfold and grow if aided by parents and teachers to express his instincts and utilize his native powers.

Froebel assumed that learning and growing merely develop already existing instincts and interests of children, who are innately good and lovable. Since he felt that he knew what those instincts and interests are, he proceeded to prescribe patterns of activity—such as predesigned games, songs, and construction projects—that would meet the educational needs of children and satisfy their spontaneous interests at their particular stages of growth. The children in his kindergarten were given simple materials—such as sand, clay, paper, cylinders, and cubes—to use in shaping designs and making objects in individual and group activities. Their imaginations were also stimulated by listening to and discussing fairy tales, stories, and legends. Froebel was further confident that the children would welcome and enthusiastically express themselves through his prearranged activities because they were drawn from their life experiences and were designed to fit into situations quite familiar to them in the home and community. In his view the activities would then be both imposed and spontaneous or creative, embracing many things the children would be thinking about and doing if left to their own resources and self-direction.

Froebel advocated manual training for older children, not for vocational reasons but rather to develop their skills and powers, an idea he was never able to implement, for there was no opportunity to organize a school for such children. The Finnish educator *Uno Cygnaeus* (1810–1888), inspired by Froebel, convinced the school authorities in Finland to introduce wood carving, metal work, and other handicrafts in 1866 as a required course for boys in the schools. In 1872 Sweden, under the leadership of *Otto Salomon* (1849–1907), modified its instructional program in carpentry and other crafts to accord with Froebelian concepts of self-development. In England, France, Russia, and Germany similar programs for boys, as well as instruction in needlework and other domestic skills for girls, were inaugurated. With various modifications, these courses spread quickly to many high schools in the United States.

Froebel's rigid, crude materials and mystical ideas were not suitable for application in schools of a later time, but his basic principles are still regarded as sound guidelines for the education of very young children. He is worthy of being ranked with his master Pestalozzi among the greatest of modern educators.

Recent and contemporary philosophers of education have sometimes merely recapitulated as if they were their own new discoveries Froebel's main pedagogical views: (1) education is not merely preparation for life, but an experience in present living that unites thought with action; (2) motor expression and learning by doing (as in gardening, needlework, weaving, music, construction, handiwork, and other self-activity) are the best methods of learning ideas, acquiring knowledge and skills, and developing powers; (3) children should be guided so that they will learn by experience in group activities to cooperate with others and form good attitudes and habits of morality, mutual aid, kindness, and friendship—all to be achieved in a kindergarten as a miniature, idealized society; (4) spontaneity, enjoyment, and reasonable, mild discipline when needed and dictated by love of children should characterize the school situation and program; and (5) the human being grows as part of nature, subject to its laws, and therefore should be studied, just as plants and animals should be studied, by teachers and scientists.

The ideas and methods of Froebel's kindergarten aroused favorable attention in the United States. In 1855 Mrs. Carl Schurz, a disciple of Froebel, organized a German-speaking kindergarten at Watertown, Wisconsin. In 1860 Elizabeth Peabody opened a private kindergarten in Boston, to be followed by the founding of a teachers' college for prospective kindergarten teachers by Matilda H. K. Kriege and Alma Kriege. Four years later Maria Kraus-Boelte established a similar training school in New York City. Susan E. Blow and the famous superintendent of schools, William Torrey Harris, organized a kindergarten for the public school system of Saint Louis in 1873. Thereafter kindergartens, as well as some training schools for kindergarten teachers, were established in urban centers of the United States. In France materials and methods of the kindergarten were made part of the program of the *écoles maternelles,* which cared for children two to six years of age. In some countries, as in England, the movement was slow because of the rapid development of infant (pre-kindergarten) schools and the founding of numerous nurseries, but the spirit of free activity characteristic of Froebel's kindergarten became a prominent feature in these schools and nurseries.

Froebel's methods of educating very young children through spontaneous activities were acclaimed by psychologists and educators as an epochal contribution to modern education. The decisive role of early childhood experience affecting the entire lifetime character of the individual was highlighted in the works of the psychoanalyst Sigmund Freud (1856–1939), the psychologists William James (1842–1910) and Arnold Lucius Gesell (1880–1961), and leading educators, such as Robert Owen (1771–1858) and Jean Piaget (1896–   ). Throughout the Western world the kindergarten changed the ideas of adults concerning the nature and needs of young children. In brief, Froebel's philosophy of education incorporated psychological and pedagogical principles that have become the core of modern educational theory and practice.

ROBERT OWEN

The industrialist, trade-union leader, philanthropist, social reformer, and educator Robert Owen (1771–1858) felt that the educational principles of Pestalozzi, Herbart, and Froebel, while useful and commendable, would be largely futile unless they were accompanied by a new form of social organization—namely, socialism. Like John Locke and Jean Jacques Rousseau, Owen brought to the center of pedagogical thought the problem of attempting to improve the school program in the face of adverse miseducating forces in society itself. He felt that social events would negate the good accomplished by the best of schools and, in the absence of a purification of society, would persist despite the heavenly rewards promised by religion or the threats posed by laws and penalties. Therefore, political, economic, and other social institutions should, in Owen's view, be reformed. Schoolteachers should be leaders, he said, in the moral regeneration and practical transformation of society, including all its institutions and enterprises, through the remaking of human character.

Since each person's character is molded by his social environment, he should not be held responsible for poverty, crime, and other social evils, which, in fact, he cannot remedy unless both education and society are perfected. All religions, Owen asserted, mistakenly blame individual sinners for immorality and human suffering and should therefore be rejected. Only the proper education of children from their earliest years and of adult workers and citizens as well can reveal the truth about the economic and social roots of evil and enable the common people to reform the moral character and the institutions of all mankind. Owen was convinced that his proposed social reforms and educational plans would create a utopian community of healthy, virtuous, enlightened, cooperative, prosperous, and happy people.

Life and Work of Robert Owen. Born in the small town of Newtown, North Wales, in 1771, Robert Owen was the precocious son of middle-class parents, his father being a saddler, iron-monger, and postmaster, a kindly yet strict disciplinarian opposed to corporal punishment of children and respectful of their judgment and personalities, an attitude shared by Robert Owen himself in later years. The boy was enrolled in a local school, where he excelled in the three Rs, music, and sports. At seven years of age he was appointed assistant teacher, thus earning enough funds to pay his own tuition. Two years thereafter he obtained employment in a drapery shop, the first step in a highly successful business career. At twenty he became manager of a mill in Manchester, England, employing five hundred workers, an experience that taught him much about the plight of the poor, aroused his sympathy, and made him determined to ameliorate their condition. Three years later he became a partner in the large Chorlton Twist Company of Manchester and, finally, in 1797 purchased with two partners the extensive cotton-spinning mills owned by his future father-in-law, David Dale, at New Lanark, Scotland.

At New Lanark, a town of 2,500 inhabitants, many of them poverty-stricken and living in unsanitary houses, Owen immediately introduced reforms. He reduced the workday in the mills to a maximum of ten and one-half hours, refused to employ children under ten years of age, ordered that the streets and houses be kept clean and in repair, stopped the sale of intoxicants, expelled profiteering retail merchants, and organized nonprofit food stores. He allocated all profits of the mills above five percent to the welfare of the workers, financing playgrounds and schools for the children. He rated the conduct and work performance of the employees and made the ratings public, thereby subjecting disorderly, lazy, or careless workers to social disapproval by the community. But Owen never punished offenders, believing that their shortcomings were attributable to misguided parents or to evil social conditions.

When Owen's partners objected to his enlightened policies, particularly to his plan to establish a new educational enterprise, the *New Institute for the Formation of Character,* to educate infants and adults, he published a defense of his proposals in four essays entitled *A New View of Society* (1813) and soon replaced these partners with more benevolent ones. He proposed remarkable modern reforms, such as old-age pensions, health insurance, free public elementary schools, community nurseries, public recreational facilities, equality of the sexes, and public housing for workers. In 1818 he visited Jean Frédéric Oberlin's infant school in France (the famous predecessor of the *écoles maternelles*), Pestalozzi's Yverdon Institute, and Fellenberg's industrial school at Hofwyl. Owen's published views and his accomplishments at New Lanark brought him worldwide acclaim; even critics who opposed his antireligious beliefs or his utopian visions respected him as a sincere idealist and humanitarian.

Owen himself, however, realized that the employees at New Lanark, despite their unprecedented successes, were still subject to his supervision and direction, not sufficiently independent or self-governing. In 1824 he and a partner, the Scottish geologist William Maclure, established a cooperative community in New Harmony, Indiana, and turned it into an experiment in common ownership of property, an attempt to implement Owen's socialist ideal of an honor system whereby each person would receive all products and services he needed in exchange for his conscientious labor.

The residents of New Harmony were a mixed group, however, many of them unprepared for such a drastic change in economic and social arrangements, or for the sudden imposition of democratic self-discipline. Disputes and dissension multiplied; Owen and Maclure quarreled about financial and educational policies; and in 1827 the experiment in cooperative living ended in disaster, leaving Owen nearly destitute. The main cause of failure was the tendency of many of the residents to substitute for Owen's ideal their own familiar motto: to each according to his desires, from each according to his fancy—the same problem that had afflicted Captain John Smith's colony of Jamestown, Virginia, in 1607, the same problem discussed in ancient times by Aristotle who, in his criticisms of Plato's communist community, pointed out that everybody's business tends to become nobody's business.

Nevertheless, through his socialist experiments, social reforms, and propaganda, Owen gave impetus to trade unionism, the cooperative movement (started as retail stores, despite Owen's doubts about their success, by Rochdale, England, pioneers in 1844), the eventual abolition of child labor, and, above all, the spread of infant schools and other facilities for the education of very young children, as well as evening schools and other schools for adults. He had hoped to organize several cooperative communities as part of a worldwide movement. But the failure in 1827 of a cooperative community founded by a disciple, Abram Combe, at Orbiston, Scotland, his own decisive disagreements with partners at New Lanark in the 1820s, the abandonment of short-lived cooperative communities in Tennessee (the Neshoba Community) and New York State (the Franklin Community), and the disaster at New Harmony in 1827, which left him without resources, limited his reformist activities to writing, lecturing, and propagandizing. His published works include *Robert Owen's Journal* (1851–1852), the *National Quarterly Review and Journal* (1853), the *Millennial Gazette* (1856–1858), and his autobiography, *The Life of Robert Owen,* written in 1857, the year before his death.

Educational Views of Robert Owen. According to Robert Owen, the development of moral character should constitute the principal aim of education. Children are plastic, moldable, potentially virtuous and intelligent human beings who will form good habits and then as adults prevent or eradicate social evils and perfect their society if correctly educated from their earliest years. Right education will remake human nature itself, transforming the masses of the poor and all others from their present stage of individual and social deficiency into an ideal, benevolent stage of brotherhood, mutual aid, self-knowledge, self-discipline, prosperity, and happiness. The poor will then be given the best possible education, heretofore available only to the rich, and a universal, democratic, purified school and society will be permanently established in cooperative communities. Eventually, said Owen, there will be no poor social classes and education will merely preserve and maintain the perfect worldwide state of humanity.

In programs for very young children attending his infant school and also for pupils five to ten years of age, Owen emphasized direct experience with animals, plants, and objects in the natural environment. He included numerous visual aids, such as maps, pictures, charts, and models, postponing the use of books, which he believed would only fill the heads of young children with words conveying information far inferior to the truths they could learn from nature itself and from discussions with teachers and one another. The life experience of children became his basis for the study of nature, human relationships, and society.

Boys and girls participated in school projects, dancing, music, and other shared activities, excepting that only boys had some military drill while girls acquired skills in sewing, cooking, and homemaking. The children were often encouraged to pursue their own interests under the kindly guidance of trained women teachers who loved and respected them, never deceived them, always expected and urged them to practice ideals of mutual aid and cooperation in play and study. Pupils ten to fifteen years old were taught practical skills, such as carpentry, homemaking, and civic duties. All children during their school years studied the three Rs, the physical and biological sciences, history, geography, modern languages, music, dancing, handwriting, and drawing, as well as technical and vocational subjects of interest to them— always emphasizing social usefulness and moral human relationships. Instruction in reading began at seven or eight years of age and was based upon the children's interests and life experiences; it included, however, selected biographies and novels. Classroom instruction, beginning with information already familiar to pupils, then advanced to new facts and their applications to life situations, stressing throughout clear comprehension of ideas and recall of supporting facts.

Owen's methods of teaching were not new, most of them being quite similar to those of Rousseau and Pestalozzi. In actual practice, as observed by Owen, Pestalozzi had often resorted to memoriter learning and other verbalistic procedures that he himself had condemned. Owen rejected the assignment of older pupils to teach younger ones, as in the monitorial system of the army chaplain Andrew Bell (1753–1832) of Madras, India, or that of the Quaker Joseph Lancaster (1778–1838) of Southwick, England, and he opposed their large classes, harsh discipline, and formalistic drill, preferring democratic self-expression, self-discipline, and spontaneous, meaningful learning experiences for children. Nevertheless, he aided Bell and Lancaster because they were sincerely attempting to spread education among the masses of the poor.

The Sunday schools originated by Robert Raikes (1735–1811) in Gloucester, England—which spread around the world as a valuable movement to extend instruction in reading, writing, and the Bible to the poor—served as means of religious indoctrination, which was anathema to Owen. Owen agreed with many of Froebel's methods of teaching but not with his religious aims, nor with Pestalozzi's admiration for mothers as ideal teachers of their own children. Owen felt that most parents miseducate or spoil their offspring, that children should be educated by trained teachers dedicated to a new social order and a new, secular cooperative society.

Owen's cooperative communities were short-lived, and many of his proposed social reforms were too far in advance of his time for wide acceptance, but the communities and reforms stimulated liberal trends in education and society in many lands. His most important immediate contribution was his influence upon the organization of infant schools by civic leaders, such as Lord Henry Peter Brougham (1778–1868), Samuel Wilderspin (1792–1866), David Stowe (1793–1864), James Pierrepont Greaves (1777–1842), and the Reverend Charles Mayo (1792–1846). But Owen's ultimate, idealistic, socialist solution to problems of human relationships, especially those among teachers, parents, leaders of churches and other social institutions, including business and government, was never widely accepted or implemented. He turned to spiritualism at eighty-two years of age, a movement to which he devoted the last five years of his career. Many of his social and educational ideals, however, have been universally admired and at least partly achieved in democracies of the Western world.

HERBERT SPENCER

The British philosopher and scholar Herbert Spencer (1820–1903) held views on the control of education and society directly contrary to Owen's socialistic doctrines. Spencer advocated rugged individualism, a laissez-faire principle that the best government is the least government, that government should do no more than is necessary to enforce legal contracts and protect the lives and property of the people from domestic violence and foreign invasion.

Spencer wrote an influential volume, *The Man Versus the State*, characterizing socialism as slavery and even condemning majority rule insofar as it interferes with individual rights and private business enterprises. As an adherent and popularizer of his friend Charles Darwin's theory of evolution and natural selection, Spencer believed in the survival of the fittest both in nature and in a competitive society and opposed centralized government control over education, economic institutions, national resources, community health facilities, or any other sphere of social welfare. He asserted that the entire universe is activated by an unknowable force (the ultimate cause of all events), which compels everything in the universe, including living organisms, to evolve from simpler and lower to more complex and higher forms of existence.

Although his own formal education was limited and he never attended a university, Spencer was descended from a family of educators and he educated himself at home, studying mathematics and the natural sciences intensively, working as an engineer and journalist, and eventually winning worldwide fame as a profound philosopher. He rejected the traditional emphasis of educators on classical studies and favored instead a broad, practical curriculum that would, he claimed, give every individual essential knowledge for complete living. He accorded the highest priority to the sciences of physiology, hygiene, chemistry, and physics as necessary means of direct self-preservation for the individual. Next to these subjects in order of importance were sciences and practical arts, useful for vocations, which provide necessities of life, thereby indirectly contributing to self-preservation. Studies helpful for the rearing and disciplining of offspring in the home ranked next in importance, followed by studies related to citizenship—that is, to political and social institutions—and then by less valuable subjects useful merely for leisure-time pursuits and enjoyments, such as literature, foreign languages, music, and fine arts.

Spencer's major contribution to education consisted of his propaganda for the physical, biological, and social sciences and practical subjects as the core of the curriculum, a point of view stated impressively in 1859 in his essay, *What Knowledge Is of Most Worth?* and elaborated in his book *Education: Intellectual, Moral, and Physical* (1861). He also claimed that the study of the sciences exercises the mind, develops mental faculties and powers, improves the memory and judgment, and fosters good habits of observation, perseverance, and respect for truth. In his *Principles of Psychology* (1855), another of his numerous comprehensive works, he attributed success in learning to the learner's interest in those things he does well and his tendency to repeat and recall pleasurable activities while avoiding or forgetting dull or painful experiences. These ideas were developed more fully as the laws of exercise (or frequency) and effect (or reinforcement and operant conditioning) by the eminent psychologists Alexander Bain (1818–1903), William James (1842–1910), Edward Lee Thorndike (1874–1949), and B. F. Skinner (1904–   ).

In his three volumes on the principles of sociology (1876, 1882, 1896), Spencer traced the evolution of social institutions (religious, industrial, and military) and even the moral sense of mankind from primitive beginnings to higher institutions and standards of modern times. Together with his scholarly contemporary Thomas H. Huxley (1825–1895), he gave strong support to the inclusion of scientific and practical subjects in the curricula of secondary and higher education. A like emphasis on science and other useful subjects—which had been previously espoused by Francis Bacon, Wolfgang Ratke, John Comenius, John Locke, and Jean Jacques Rousseau—was recommended by later educators, notably by the Scottish phrenologist George Combe (1788–1858), the American statesman and educational reformer Horace Mann (1796–1859), the president of Brown University Francis Wayland (1796–1865), the American author and lecturer Edward L. Youmans (1821–1887), and the famous president of Harvard University Charles William Eliot (1834–1926). Spencer, however, in contrast to many other leading educators, greatly undervalued the worth of emotional and aesthetic experiences of learners. Huxley's view of the curriculum was much broader than Spencer's and emphasized history, government, ethics, language and literature, music, and the fine arts as well as the sciences.

HORACE MANN

Horace Mann was a brilliant attorney, statesman, and educator credited with being the greatest of the founders of the American public school system, a practical-minded eloquent spokesman for the cause of free, universal, nonsectarian education. Unlike Spencer, he was concerned mainly with educational practices rather than profound philosophical theory.

Career of Horace Mann. Born in the farming town of Franklin, Massachusetts, in 1796, Mann attended the local one-room school, in which he learned the three Rs, the catechism, and little else, but in his teens he was tutored in Greek and Latin by an itinerant schoolmaster and in geometry by a Baptist minister, enabling him to pass the examination for admission to Brown University (in Providence, Rhode Island). At the university he excelled in his studies, concentrating on classical languages, geography, logic, and public speaking. Upon graduation he worked briefly in a law office and tutored students at the university. In 1821 he enrolled in a Connecticut law school as the first step in a successful legal career, and in 1827 he won election to the Massachusetts legislature, serving six years in the state house of representatives and four years in the state senate. He argued effectively for religious liberty, for government aid to industry, and for humane treatment of prisoners and the insane, and as president of the state senate he was mainly responsible for the establishment of the first state hospital for the insane in the nation.

As president of the state senate he also successfully supported James G. Carter's bill to establish the first state Board of Education. In 1837 he resigned from the senate in order to serve as the first Secretary of that Board, an office he held until 1848. From 1837 to 1848, he issued annual reports on Massachusetts schools, reports that aroused the people of the state to demand the im-

provement, consolidation, financial support, expansion, and reform of the public schools as indispensable, free, universal,
nonsectarian institutions and pillars of American democracy.
Contributing some of his own funds, Mann induced the state to
organize three highly efficient normal schools for training prospective teachers. He investigated conditions in home, school, and
public libraries. Through the influence of Governor De Witt
Clinton (1769–1828), proponent of tax-supported public schools
and state aid for teacher training, New York State in 1835 had
appropriated tax moneys for school libraries, and a similar enact-
ment passed in Massachusetts in 1837. Mann insisted that all
books in public school libraries be nonsectarian in accordance
with the Constitutional separation of church and state. In 1839
he founded a semimonthly periodical, *The Massachusetts
Common School Journal,* to propagandize for public education.
He became a prominent exponent and leader of the movement
for free, universal, tax-supported public schools throughout the
United States. In 1843 he toured in Europe and studied the
educational systems of Great Britain, Germany, and France, and
upon his return recommended many of the German procedures
as well as some of the others in his *Seventh Annual Report* of
that year. His criticisms of the Massachusetts schools aroused
spirited opposition among Boston schoolmasters, who defended
their traditional dependence on textbooks as primary tools of
instruction, the alphabetic method of teaching reading (instead
of the whole-word method advocated by Mann), corporal punishment, and sectarian religion in the schools, but Mann succeeded
in introducing needed reforms in these practices.

In 1848, however, he resigned his position as Secretary of the
state Board of Education to succeed John Quincy Adams as a
member of the United States House of Representatives. He condemned and antagonized Daniel Webster because Webster was
willing to accept Henry Clay's proposed compromise on the extension of slavery. Mann was a steadfast abolitionist who predicted that the southern states would be defeated in a civil war if
they attempted to secede from the Union on the slavery issue.

In 1852 Mann lost the election for governor of Massachusetts.
Thereafter he served as president of a new coeducational college,

Antioch College, in Yellow Springs, Ohio, until his death in 1859. Characteristically, during his presidency at Antioch College, he insisted on the admission of students irrespective of race, creed, or sex.

Horace Mann's Educational Views.   Mann perceived the need for convincing the general public about the true value of free, universal education under the direction of competent, trained teachers as an instrument for preserving and ensuring the success and prosperity of a democratic nation. Among his predecessors who had similarly propagandized for American public education were the Reverend Thomas Hopkins Gallaudet (1787–1851), who wrote numerous articles in behalf of normal schools for prospective teachers and introduced the manual method of teaching the deaf; the Reverend Samuel Read Hall (1795–1877), the writer of school textbooks who organized normal schools at Concord, Vermont, Andover, Massachusetts, and Plymouth, New Hampshire; and James G. Carter (1795–1849), who sponsored effective laws for tax-supported high schools and normal schools, especially the Massachusetts law of 1827 initiating the public high school movement.

But it was Mann who, as Secretary of the Massachusetts Board of Education, dealt with all major phases of needed educational reforms, defending Pestalozzi's method of instruction in the humanities and sciences and stressing the need for centralization and efficient management of schools. He pleaded for a practical curriculum of useful subjects, the organization of more high schools, coeducation, higher salaries and equal pay for men and women teachers, teachers' institutes and normal schools, health education and a healthier environment in the schools, a longer school term, and adequate supervision of teaching.

Mann regarded moral character, effective citizenship, and practical efficiency in life as the highest educational aims, meriting priority in the school program. He appealed for the adaptation of teaching methods to the interests and individual differences of pupils, for the inductive method, and for emphasis upon comprehension and understanding instead of memoriter or rote learning. He condemned the traditional district system of local control over the schools as a system penalizing poorer communities and perpetuating inefficient, unpopular, and impractical instruction, and he advocated state aid and control to ensure high standards of nonsectarian public education throughout the state. He favored sympathetic treatment of pupils, nondenominational teaching of religious ideals, and the separation of public education from partisan politics. He originated no new philosophy of education, but he disseminated widely the views and recommendations of great modern educators, and he implemented many of them in educational practice.

HENRY BARNARD

There is a remarkable similarity between the careers, views, and educational contributions of Horace Mann and those of Henry Barnard. Like Mann, Barnard was a native New Englander, born in a farming family (in Hartford, Connecticut, in 1811) and educated in inferior local schools. In his teens he studied the classics and literature, as Mann did, under the direction of competent scholars, and at fifteen years of age was admitted to Yale University where he, again like Mann, excelled in his studies, which included classical languages and public speaking. He graduated in 1830 at the age of nineteen. Barnard developed admiration of Pestalozzi's views on education, studied law, taught students, worked as an assistant librarian, and, having been admitted to the Connecticut bar in 1835, began a legal career.

In 1837 he followed Mann's example by being elected to the state legislature, sponsoring in that body liberal legislation in behalf of prisoners, the insane, and handicapped citizens, propagandizing for public libraries and laws for the improvement of public education, and serving as secretary of the state Board of Commissioners of Common Schools (1838–1842, 1851–1855). Like Mann, he edited famous educational publications (*The Connecticut Common School Journal,* 1838–1842, 1852–1855; *The Journal of the Rhode Island Institute of Instruction,* 1845–1849; and *The American Journal of Education,* 1855–1881, consisting of thirty-one volumes), traveled widely in Europe to observe school systems, defended the role and status of women teachers, initiated teachers' institutes (in Connecticut, Wisconsin, and Rhode Island), and evangelized for many years, until his death in 1900, in behalf of tax-supported, nonpartisan, nonsectarian public education and normal schools for training competent teachers. From 1843 to 1849 he served in Rhode Island as state superintendent of schools, from 1850 to 1855 in Connecticut as state superintendent of schools, from 1859 to 1861 as chancellor of the University of Wisconsin, from 1866 to 1867 as president of Saint John's College in Annapolis, Maryland, and from 1867 to 1870 as the first United States commissioner of education.

On political and social issues, Barnard was more conservative than most of the great educators in modern times, far more conservative than Rousseau, Owen, and other leading social reformers. In his writings he defended the capitalist system and private enterprise, admired wealthy contributors to charitable causes, and attributed the poverty of the poor to personality defects; yet he also insisted that the wealthy classes should encourage and assist in the provision of good common schools and adequate housing for the poor.

In his pedagogical views, Barnard followed the example of Horace Mann, advocating the Pestalozzian emphasis on life experience, activities, and practical subjects in the elementary and secondary schools of the nation, influential views effectively propounded in his epochal *American Journal of Education* (supported in part by his own funds), which became a sourcebook and guide in the development of education in America and in many other countries, embracing every phase of instruction, including kindergartens, elementary and high schools, technical and industrial schools, teacher education, college education, the education of minorities and delinquents, curricula, the psychology of learning, methods of teaching, and school organization and supervision.

Barnard was particularly concerned about educational opportunities for women. Emma Willard had organized a seminary for women in Troy, New York, in 1821, and Mary Lyon had founded Mount Holyoke Seminary for girls in South Hadley, Massachusetts, in 1836. The old, declining Latin grammar schools had excluded girls, but the burgeoning academies had begun to admit them and were becoming coeducational. Barnard felt that women could never develop into efficient mothers and homemakers unless they were broadly educated, and he was proud of having employed many women as teachers in Rhode Island who had greatly improved the morale and accomplishments of the schools in that state.

Finally, as the first United States Commissioner of Education, he initiated statistical surveys of school and college programs and achievements. When political opposition resulted in the abolition of the Department of Education in 1868, he soon thereafter resigned from government service and devoted himself to editing the *American Journal of Education* until it ceased publication in 1881.

CHARLES WILLIAM ELIOT

Another influential modern educator, Charles William Eliot, followed the example of Spencer, Huxley, Mann, and Barnard in attempting to reform deficient means and methods of public education, particularly through a new emphasis upon scientific and practical subjects in the curriculum, adaptation of instruction to individual interests and capacities, and encouragement of increased independence and freedom of choice, self-direction, and self-discipline of the student population.

Eliot credited scientific discoveries, inventions, and methods of investigation with much of the progress achieved by political, industrial, and educational institutions of the nineteenth and early twentieth centuries. As a conservative reformer, he believed that educational institutions, especially business departments of universities, should fit into and foster the growth of the free, competitive, economic enterprises of the nation. He advocated nature study as a major subject in the earliest grades of elementary school and the selection of teachers well versed in the physical and biological sciences.

Born in Boston in 1834 into a prestigious family, his father having been mayor of Boston and a congressman, Eliot, though troubled by physical ailments in his childhood and youth, graduated from Harvard College in 1853 and immediately joined the faculty as tutor and later (1858–1863) as assistant professor of chemistry. He served as professor of chemistry at the new university, the Massachusetts Institute of Technology, from 1865 to 1869, at which time he was elected president of Harvard University, a post he filled with brilliant success for the next forty years of his career.

Eliot was a tactful strategist, a liberal, democratic, but gradualist reformer in education who did not join in the extremist claims of science educators for the assumed superiority of scientific studies over classical subjects as mental disciplines, and he was himself a graduate of the Boston Latin Grammar School (which Benjamin Franklin also attended) and editor of the Harvard Classics, a five-foot shelf of philosophical, scientific, and literary masterpieces.

He was mainly responsible for the extension of the elective system in American colleges, the establishment of higher standards of scholarship in secondary schools through stricter college entrance requirements, the unification of the college curriculum, greater emphasis upon English composition, and the introduction of programs whereby high school students uninterested in college could be prepared for commercial and industrial careers. His address at the 1892 meeting of the National Education Association advocated diversity (as well as some uniformity) in public schools in order to meet the individual needs and interests of pupils, a view that gave impetus to the movement for adaptation of instruction to individual differences among learners. His advocacy of an enriched curriculum in elementary schools invigorated the movement for the organization of junior high schools. At Harvard University he introduced the precedent-setting elective system (later modified and restricted during the years 1909 to 1933 by his highly conservative successor Abbott Lawrence Lowell), integrated the college with graduate and professional schools, organized a graduate school in the arts and sciences, established nonsectarian principles in the divinity school, and raised standards of instruction in the law and medical schools. He appointed to the faculty of Harvard College the great educator William James (1842–1910); the philosopher, classicist, and educator George Herbert Palmer (1842–1933); the prominent theologian Edward Caldwell Moore (1857–1943); the noted psychologist Hugo Munsterberg (1863–1916); the leading economist of his time, Frank William Taussig (1859–1940); the world-famous Shakespearian scholar, George Lyman Kittredge (1860–1941); and the renowned linguist and Dante authority, Charles Hall Grandgent (1862–1939). Intensely interested in the higher education of women, he assisted in the founding of Radcliffe College (for women) in Cambridge, Massachusetts. In many respects his views paved the way for a new, democratic spirit on all levels of education best suited to the needs of the developing industrial society of the American republic.

The wisdom and sterling character of Charles William Eliot manifested themselves during the 1920s, when the Harvard University authorities, in response to the recommendation of President Lowell, Eliot's successor, approved a *numerus clausus,* limiting the number of Jewish and other minority applicants for admission.* But Eliot, at the age of ninety-one, visited minority students at Harvard College and urged them to remain proud of their heritage, stating that Lowell's un-American policy would not prevail, and the policy was in fact soon reversed.

AMERICAN UNIVERSITY EDUCATORS

In higher education Eliot was one of the most influential contributors in a long list of distinguished leaders, including Benjamin Franklin (1706–1790), who recommended the establishment of the University of Pennsylvania (opened in 1751); Thomas Jefferson (1743–1826), president of the United States (1801–1809),

---

* Lowell unsuccessfully opposed President Woodrow Wilson's appointment in 1916 of the Jewish attorney and labor-union advocate Louis Dembitz Brandeis to the United States Supreme Court. In 1927 he served on the committee appointed by Massachusetts Governor Alvin T. Fuller that ruled against Sacco and Vanzetti, anarchists accused of murder and sentenced to death by an obviously biased jurist, Judge Webster Thayer. The judge's threats both in and out of the courtroom, proving that he had deprived Sacco and Vanzetti of a fair trial, were never disclosed by Lowell, not even in his sealed papers, finally opened in 1977, which categorized Thayer's remarks as being merely "a grave breach of official decorum." In 1977 Governor Michael S. Dukakis of Massachusetts apologized for the judicial murder of the two anarchists.

a founder of the University of Virginia (chartered in 1819); Francis Wayland (1796–1865), influential advocate of science studies, president of Brown University (1827–1855); Daniel Coit Gilman (1831–1908), librarian, geographer, president of the University of California (1872–1875) and president of the Johns Hopkins University (1875–1901); Andrew Dickson White (1832–1918), famous diplomat, organizer with Ezra Cornell (1807–1874) and president of Cornell University (1868–1885); Henry Mitchell MacCracken (1840–1918), clergyman, philosopher, chancellor of New York University (1891–1910); Granville Stanley Hall (1844–1924), noted psychologist, president of Clark University (1889–1919); William Rainey Harper (1856–1906), first president of the University of Chicago (1891–1906); Woodrow Wilson (1856–1924), president of Princeton University (1902–1910) and President of the United States (1915–1921); Booker T. Washington (1856–1915), founder and first president of Tuskegee Institute (1881); Nicholas Murray Butler (1862–1947), recipient of the Nobel peace prize (1931) and president of Columbia University (1902–1945); William Allan Neilson (1869–1946), editor-in-chief of *Webster's International Dictionary,* Second Edition (1934) and president of Smith College (1917–1939); James R. Angell (1869–1949), eminent psychologist, president of Yale University (1921–1937); Alexander Meiklejohn (1872–1964), experimental educator at the University of Wisconsin (1926–1933), president of Amherst College (1912–1919); James Bryant Conant (1893–1978), diplomat, like Eliot a chemist and reformer of public high school programs, a defender of free speech for campus and faculty radicals, a liberal scientist who succeeded Abbott Lawrence Lowell as president of Harvard University (1933–1953); and Robert Maynard Hutchins (1899–   ), humanist, liberal sponsor of classical learning and philosophy in a great-books program, defender of free speech and academic freedom, and president (1929–1945) and chancellor (1945–1951) of the University of Chicago.

Among Eliot's successors as president of Harvard University, James B. Conant merits special commendation for his innovations in secondary and higher education. He advocated scholarships for economically disadvantaged students; pure research by college and university faculty members; the extension and enrichment of foreign-language courses in secondary schools; racial integration; practical education and employment opportunities for minority youths; stimulation of intrinsic interest in studies instead of academic degrees; increased federal aid to education and tighter state control over local expenditures for education; a counseling system to advise pupils from the earliest grades through senior high school; individualized programs of study; required courses in English, government, mathematics, and science; greater use of ability grouping of students; full reporting on each pupil's progress throughout his high school years; coordination of vocational education with economic conditions and institutions in each community; and special aid to students retarded in reading and gifted students.

In American higher education generally, during the third quarter of the twentieth century, Harvard, Columbia, Princeton, Yale, Chicago, California, and other leading universities maintained close relationships with federal government agencies, becoming increasingly involved in numerous government-financed research programs, as well as military and civilian projects of large dimensions, including an intimate relationship between faculty members and national domestic and foreign policies. Physicists at the universities developed military devices and techniques; engineering and business schools, public health and medical schools, and law schools contributed advice and personnel on a fee basis for many government programs; while federal government appropriations and loans to students helped to meet the continually increasing costs of instruction, equipment, research, and personnel. (Government funds also assisted technical and vocational schools as well as public elementary and secondary academic schools.) Local governments built and financed hundreds of two-year community colleges and junior colleges, characterized too frequently by low academic standards but generally useful for training students for commercial, industrial, and subprofessional occupations.

The prestige of leading American universities was adversely affected by scandals growing out of faculty connections with the Vietnam War, especially during the years 1965 to 1972 (in 1970 one hundred colleges closed in demonstrations against the war and the killing of four protesting students at Kent State University, Ohio, by national guardsmen). Corrupt political practices involving numerous law school graduates serving in the tragic presidency of Richard Nixon further eroded this prestige, along with widespread indications of a low level of ethics and a high level of greed among university graduates prominent in the economic, political, legal, and medical professions. Furthermore, the possibility of reduced allotments for aid to education in national and state budgets coupled with the danger of a potential decline in enrollments and income at private and public colleges, which were already beset by rising costs of operation, increased uncertainty about the future course of higher education.

JOHN DEWEY AND HERMAN HARREL HORNE

Two of the most influential and highly respected educational theorists in American universities during the first half of the twentieth century were John Dewey (1859–1952), who taught at the University of Minnesota (1888–1889), the University of Michigan (1889–1894), the University of Chicago (1894–1904), and Columbia University (1904–1952), and Herman Harrel Horne (1874–1946), who taught at New York University (1908–1942). Dewey was an adherent of the pragmatist views expounded by the mathematician and profound logician Charles Sanders Peirce (1839–1914) and the eminent psychologist and philosopher William James (1842–1910) of Harvard University, whereas Horne was a religious idealist who recapitulated the principal idealist concepts of Josiah Royce (1855–1916) and William Ernest Hocking (1873–1966), both world-renowned philosophers of Harvard University.

Educational Views of John Dewey. Dewey wrote numerous works elaborating on a complex pragmatic philosophy, which he identified with his theory of education. He emphasized the same ideas about learning through activity and child-centered instruction advocated during the eighteenth and early nineteenth centuries by Pestalozzi and Froebel. A number of similar ideas had been expounded by Colonel Francis Wayland Parker (1837–1902), principal of the Cook County Normal School of Chicago. The most representative feature of Dewey's philosophy of education was his recommendation of the project method of learning, described by various followers as a purposive, problem-solving activity carried on in its natural setting. Dewey's theories were popularized mainly by William Heard Kilpatrick (1871–1965), a colleague at Teachers College of Columbia University, who lectured eloquently to thousands of teachers and converted many of them into proponents of the *progressive education movement*, which became widely influential in American schools and abroad during the third, fourth, and fifth decades of the twentieth century. Another prolific writer and proponent of Dewey's philosophy and of scientific procedures for curriculum reconstruction was Harold Ordway Rugg (1886–1960), author of numerous popular works on the merits and defects of American culture and civilization.

Teachers College of Columbia University gained considerable prestige from the works of numerous eminent psychologists during the first half of the twentieth century, including Robert Sessions Woodworth (1869–1962), research psychologist in learning, motivation, and reasoning; Edward Lee Thorndike (1874–1949), specialist in animal and human learning processes; Harry Levi Hollingworth (1880–1956), researcher in vocational and personnel psychology and in abnormal psychology; Rudolf Pintner (1884–1942), pioneer in the psychology of handicapped children and originator of tests of intelligence and motor performance; Arthur Irving Gates (1890–1972), noted author of reading tests and specialist in the psychology of reading; Percival Mallon Symonds (1893–1960), well-known clinical psychologist; Gardner Murphy (1895–   ), eminent social psychologist; and George Wilfried Hartmann (1904–1955), prominent educational psychologist and social psychologist, exponent of Gestalt psychology. In addition, the writings of Paul Monroe (1869–1947) of Teachers College, ranking with Ellwood P. Cubberley (1868–1941) of the University of California as a leading historian of education, contributed to the high reputation of the institution. Teachers College became the most popular national institution for the training of teachers and a center of nationwide propaganda for John Dewey's philosophy of education.

According to Dewey's theory of purposive activity or the successful completion of projects as the ideal method of learning, (1) the learner must become inherently interested in a potentially educative activity, experience, or situation; (2) he must locate and define a difficulty, perplexity, or problem to be solved; (3) he must collect pertinent data through memory, reasoning, and personal experience or research; (4) he must determine possible solutions to the difficulty, perplexity, or problem to be solved; and (5) he must test the best possible solutions through application in experience, experiments, and everyday life. In the learning process the student should concentrate on the main problem to be solved; he should be open-minded and accept all reasonable sources of information and suggestions; he should remain interested in the problem itself and its possible solution, not in the extraneous advantages or disadvantages that might ensue; and he should then accept all the consequences of his conclusions and decisions.

Dewey criticized Herbart and his disciples for a rigid, excessive formalism and for the formulation of the Herbartian five steps of learning (preparation, presentation, comparison, generalization, and application). Yet Dewey's own five steps were strikingly formal and similar in approach despite his emphasis on problem-solving instead of the Herbartian goal of mastery of ideas. Dewey allowed the pupil much greater freedom to choose activities, and he advocated individualized instruction as well as social participation by the pupil in group projects. (In 1920 at Dalton, Massachusetts, Helen Parkhurst originated the temporarily popular Dalton Plan of individual instruction, in which pupil and teacher enter into a contract calling for mastery of specific lessons, problems, or activities. In Winnetka, Illinois, similar individualized instruction was supplemented by group activities in the Winnetka Plan, developed by Carleton W. Washburne.)

Dewey believed that public education, properly administered, could improve society, that the ideal school should be a miniature, purified society of its own, that education should develop fully the individual's interests and abilities so that he will participate efficiently in his school and community, that the student should make use of construction, tools, games and play, observation of nature, self-expression (not mere obedience to other people), and purposive activities as the proper means of learning and self-development, that students should learn about social institutions and ways of living by means of reasonable participation and work in school and community, and, finally, that education exists to perpetuate the institutions, customs, skills, and knowledge transmitted from one generation to succeeding generations.

The Educational Philosophy of Herman Harrel Horne. Herman Harrel Horne approved of many of Dewey's suggestions, including the emphasis on projects and activities as useful means of education, but he also pointed out serious limitations and deficiencies in Dewey's point of view, especially in regard to pursuing projects for relatively insignificant purposes or neglecting moral standards and precepts. According to Horne, Dewey himself, while he rejected lecturing to students as a teaching method, exerted his influence mainly by lecturing others about his ideas, not by demonstrating them in practice (with the exception of initial experiments at the University of Chicago from 1896 to 1903). Dewey admitted his indebtedness for many of his pragmatic pedagogical suggestions to preceding great educators, such as Pestalozzi and Froebel, whom he criticized chiefly for their mystical or idealist views.

Horne declared that Dewey overemphasized the social aspects of education by ignoring the individual's need of privacy, personal ideals and visions, and inspirations or insights only remotely connected with problems to be solved. For Horne, the most potent forces in education are the traditional ethical ideals of the great religious prophets and seers, the moral principles in the Ten Commandments and other biblical teachings—for a people without vision must indeed perish from the earth. Thus, many of the most valued acquisitions, discoveries, and accomplishments of mankind came about through sudden inspiration or insight, sympathy and affection immediately awakened, and even through subject-matter learning and lecturing rejected by Dewey, not always through activities and occupations or projects. The child, said Horne, is always the center of his own learning process whether or not he is active or merely reflective at any particular time. It was Froebel who reminded us that thinking is in itself a vital activity for its own sake. Horne declared that thinking and feeling have immense educational value before, during, and after activities and also quite apart from activities.

It seemed to Horne that the pragmatic, project method had failed to produce convincing evidence of substantial improvements in either the moral character or the knowledge, skills, and powers of individual pupils. (Scholars favoring Dewey's point of view conducted an eight-year study of results among high school students in the 1930s and claimed some advantages for the activity method but no startling achievements.) In fact, a reaction against progressive education set in during the latter part of the twentieth century, as the American culture continued to be characterized by excessive competition, ever-increasing crime rates, greed, political corruption, international strife, war, and social instability—the very same evils that the scientific, problem-solving methods of research and instruction had been designed to eradicate. The pragmatic philosophy, even in its relatively limited applications, seemed to have failed its own test of definite, practical success. It became obvious, moreover, that none of the various pragmatic and idealist philosophies of education had produced a likely prospect of effective remedies for the basic defects and problems of modern society. Some defeatist critics even began to condemn public education itself.

At Columbia University, during the anticommunist, antiradical campaigns of congressional committees in the late 1940s and 1950s, internal dissension and devious political tactics, together with the passing of many eminent faculty members, considerably diminished the previously decisive influence of its Teachers College, which, however, continued to attract large numbers of teachers to its training programs. During the 1930s and 1940s an essentialist school of thought at the college, a small minority led by William Chandler Bagley (1874–1946), attempted to counteract Dewey's point of view through a traditional emphasis on subject-matter learning and the development of ideals as the primary aims of education. The influential Council for Basic Education was founded by conservative educators in 1956 to disseminate the essentialist philosophy of education.

At the New York University School of Education, a number of faculty members approved of major aspects of John Dewey's philosophy of education, while others agreed with Herman Harrel Horne's idealist views. The renowned specialist in experimental education, Paul Rankov Radosavljevich, who had been an associate of the famous German educational psychologist and anthropologist Ernst Meumann (1862–1915) and had added new experimental findings to researches on memory by Herman Ebbinghaus (1850–1909), introduced courses in experimental education (1910–1944) and stressed the need for genuine experimentation that would apply the various approaches and proposed techniques of instruction in a natural classroom setting, but nowhere in the United States (or elsewhere) were such scientific experiments undertaken. (The "experimental" or "model" schools at universities and teachers' colleges designed their activities mainly to demonstrate preconceived concepts or philosophies of education.) The New York University idealist educational administrator John W. Withers, who had been a pioneering superintendent of schools in Saint Louis, Missouri, built a remarkable record of achievement at the university school of education. (Withers joined his distinguished colleague Albert B. Meredith, former Commissioner of Education in the state of Connecticut, in stressing the need for a great expansion of two-year colleges decades before the large network of community colleges evolved.) The extraordinary accomplishments of its faculty during the 1930s, 1940s, and 1950s enabled New York University to continue to attract large numbers of teachers in all fields of education, with large enrollments in the unprecedented courses of Robert K. Speer, Alice V. Keliher, H. H. Giles, Dan W. Dodson, Theodore Brameld, and William Van Til in education for human relations and racial integration. (In 1954 the United States Supreme Court declared school segregation to be unconstitutional in deciding five legal cases in *Brown et al.* v. *Board of Education of Topeka et al.,* accepting the convincing arguments of the noted jurists Thurgood Marshall and Constance Baker Motley that segregation deprives black students of reasonably equal protection of the laws guaranteed to all American citizens by the Fourteenth Amendment to the Constitution. The following year the court held that a "prompt and reasonable start" must be made to end such segregation with "all deliberate speed." During the 1960s and 1970s numerous private schools were organized for children of anti-integrationists both in the southern states and in some urban districts of the North. Thousands of church schools were also founded by conservative religionists to implement the beliefs of their adherents in strict order, thorough discipline, and intensive study of denominational religion and traditional school subjects.)

ALTERNATIVE PHILOSOPHIES OF EDUCATION

In the late nineteenth and twentieth centuries, various alternative philosophies of education were being proposed by leading educators in addition to those of the pragmatist Dewey and the idealist Horne and their numerous followers. The Russian literary genius Count Leo Nikolaevich Tolstoi (1828–1910) conducted an extraordinary religiously motivated school on his country estate, Yasnaja Polyana, teaching the value of self-sacrifice, love of humanity beginning with one's nearest neighbors, and nonviolent resistance to evil as the ideal aims of education. Alfred North Whitehead (1861–1947), brilliant mathematician and philosopher at Cambridge University and later at Harvard University, concluded that the activity of the human mind has the highest value among all events in the universe, a value to be found in, but not restricted to, successful occupations, skills, or projects, nor even to subject-matter mastery and scientific investigations. Thus Whitehead's philosophy of education returned full circle, after more than two thousand years, to the conflict between Plato's characterization of pure ideas as the supreme good and Aristotle's concept of reason as the most distinctive, useful, specific, and satisfying experience of mankind. For Whitehead knowledge and the expert practical application of knowledge are both necessary. Similarly, the British philosopher Bertrand Arthur William Russell (1872–1970), coauthor with Whitehead of the three-volume *Principia Mathematica* (1910–1913), felt that knowledge, as such, though valuable, is not enough for humanity, that creative impulses, free self-expression, and social cooperation and approval by one's fellowmen are essential aims of education.

The personalist philosophy of Martin Buber (1878–1965), the

Jewish theologian sympathetic to Christian philosophy, distinguished between rational, inductive scientific knowledge and the actual experience of human beings in their relationships to nature, to beauty, and to other people. Nature can be studied, analyzed, described, in part controlled, but it can also be appreciated by man as something beautiful, as an inner experience of the individual. The development of spontaneous respect and sympathy for others, fostering each person's sense of freedom and the sharing of visions and hopes with fellow human beings, are the proper aims of education. Institutions and social structures may be changed in one direction or another; they may even become arbitrary and antagonistic; but the individual learner, said Buber, can still find self-direction and personal liberty through human love and companionship. The Existentialist philosopher Sören Kierkegaard (1813–1855) believed that every person passes through life stages of pleasure-seeking, ethical commitment and decision making, and, finally, religious self-awareness and faith in man as part of a never-ending universe—that, therefore, faith in God is the ultimate aim of growth in learning and being. The atheist Existentialist philosopher Jean-Paul Sartre (1905–   ) substituted for such faith a sense of personal freedom as the ultimate aim of education and existence. Other complex philosophies—for example, that of Rudolf Steiner (1861–1925), the Austrian founder of anthroposophy—espoused the relationship of complete sympathy, rapport, and kindness between teacher and student as the secret of effective education. Numerous enthusiastic adherents found an element of truth and practical value in these divergent philosophies.

The educational philosophy of the Italian Neo-Hegelian philosopher and educator Giovanni Gentile (1875–1944), director of education in Italy during 1922 and 1923, and the similar views of the noted Italian philosopher Benedetto Croce (1866–1952) condemned modern curricula and teaching methods that depend on pragmatic or materialistic success of pupils and scientific analysis of the learning process. Gentile believed in a spiritual relationship between pupils and teacher whereby the teacher strives to understand the true character and mental experiences of each pupil. Teacher and pupil should, he asserted, together decide on each new learning experience, and the learner should feel free and creative yet be subject to correction and redirection whenever the teacher, aided by his rich background of life and teaching experience, determines that the pupil needs such guidance in order to develop further his moral and spiritual ideals and character.

Finally, the instructional programs of Maria Montessori (1870–1952), the Italian physician and educator, have been of great significance, as have the researches of Arnold Lucius Gesell (1880–1961) and the Swiss child psychologist Jean Piaget (1896–). Taking her cue from the renowned French physician Édouard Seguin (1812–1880), Montessori devised special means and methods of educating defectives and mentally retarded children in Rome and eventually applied similar approaches in teaching normal children, emphasizing pupils' intiative, sensory and muscular exercises and games, and guided self-activities, which are to be carefully observed and evaluated by the teacher. Pupils are given a large measure of freedom to solve their own problems and fulfill their own interests subject to rules of conduct and the practical requirements of life situations. Many lessons and experiences, however, are preplanned, and pupils are expected to complete tasks satisfactorily in order to develop their sensory awareness and judgment. Sensory training precedes the acquisition of entire skills in writing, reading, and arithmetic. The Montessori methods have therefore been criticized for failing to provide pupils with enough opportunities to create their own tasks instead of being required to complete those assigned to them by the teacher. Nevertheless, in some respects the Montessori methods and the atmosphere of free self-direction often prevailing are reminiscent of Pestalozzian and Froebelian ideas, but on a more individualized, experimental, formal, scientific basis. The investigations and findings during the 1930s to 1960s of the child psychologist Gesell and his colleagues at Yale University contributed detailed information concerning the physical, mental, motor, and linguistic growth and development of infants and young children. Still more recently, Jean Piaget studied the intellectual development of the child, especially progress in his awareness of ideas, such as ideas of space and time, cause and effect, and number relationships. According to Piaget, it takes considerable time, for example, for a child to develop his awareness of the difference between a whole object and its various parts. The experiments of the Harvard University psychologist B. F. Skinner (1904–   ) in operant conditioning and reinforcement of learning—reminiscent of Pavlov's theories of the conditioned reflex and Thorndike's laws of readiness, exercise, and effect—have aroused considerable interest among contemporary educators, especially as applied in technical and vocational training. All these avenues of research may, it is hoped, increase the efficacy of instruction and supplement the pragmatic and idealist programs of education designed by great educators as means of remaking, enriching, and ennobling human nature itself.

CONCLUSION

The great educators of modern times, heeding the lessons of ancient and medieval history, have counseled parents and teachers wisely, but too few people have adequately comprehended or implemented their recommendations. Consequently their ideals, moral standards, and highest aspirations have largely failed to achieve for mankind the true values of universal liberty, justice, brotherhood, peace, and good will, all the indispensable elements required for material, social, and spiritual fulfillment. Each of the great educators has contributed invaluable insights and suggestions, which teachers can and should apply to the improvement of education. Every teacher should make use of this heritage of ideas, adapting selected goals and means of instruction to the intellectual and moral needs of individual children. Even more important, teachers and parents should realize that the cultural deprivation of a single child in our modern world brings irreparable loss to all humanity. No nation, no community, no individual in our time can become secure, virtuous, prosperous, happy, and truly successful without striving to advance the welfare, freedom, and self-direction, the material, intellectual, and spiritual interests, of all children in all lands.

The great educators labored not for one social class or region but for all mankind. Let us resolve that they shall not have labored in vain.

INDEX